DBT Skills Workbook for Beginners

Easy to Learn DBT Skills for Managing
Anxiety, Depression, Anger, and BPD

Linda Hill

Table of Contents

Introduction

You can live well with a mental illness. It may take time, but it's worth it. You deserve to live a happy and healthy life.
−Demi Lovato

Many of us plow through life as best we can. We are able to stay strong through any hard times or adversity thrown our way and to keep moving forward. We are aware of when to reach out and when that bump needs a bit more help to get over than we can scale on our own. Whether that looks like reaching out to an individual in our support network, turning to a spirit guide, or seeking therapeutic insight, it's knowing when a situation is bigger than you feel strong enough to face alone and accepting outside help. Some of us, though, may not embrace this concept as easily.

Even in these modern times where there is so much emphasis

placed on the importance of practicing optimal health, which is the combination of mental, physical, emotional, and spiritual health, the area that is criticized and riddled with judgment the most is our mental health. Because of the stigma that's placed on those living with mental health struggles, there are people who live with serious conditions they either ignore, hide, or deny just so they "fit in" to how society feels one should behave. Several conditions can become all-consuming when not treated effectively. This is devastating when we consider that in many of these situations all the individual needs is a well-suited therapy treatment in conjunction with medication to live a full and successful live. This is where DBT can become, literally, a life-saving practice for many individuals.

Both the individual who is struggling, as well as those who love them, can gain tremendous benefits from this cognitive behavior therapy. It's designed to teach people a new set of skills to draw from in order to regulate their thoughts, emotions, and behaviors in specific situations more effectively. These skills will not just help the individual live a happier life, they will also teach family, friends, and other loved ones how to use DBT to support the individual. Until those living with personality, mood, or behavioral disorders get the kind of help specific to their condition, it can be heartbreaking not to understand how to truly support them.

By embracing DBT skills, individuals will be able to

- Control their unhealthy impulses, no matter what the trigger is

- Learn how to organize themselves to tackle tasks at hand, or simply get through each day

- Understand how to self-regulate, even when the emotions, thoughts, or memories are extremely intense

- Refocus their attention on where it needs to be, rather than on the trigger

For those of us who've lived with and loved a person with a serious mental health condition, and who have seen, cared for, or been with them through the worst of the worst times, these points may seem too simplistic to be attainable. This isn't to say the process will be a "quick fix" or easy. It will definitely take a lot of hard work, patience, and perseverance, but it's possible.

Each chapter will contain discussions, as well as strategies, tips, and exercises, that focus on five main skill areas that need to be strengthened and maintained:

- **Mindfulness:** This is a main component as those who struggle with mental issues are "stuck" in the past, making moving forward difficult. This mindset is the practice of being fully aware and present in any given moment.

- **Emotional regulation:** This is also a big one because some individuals lose control of their emotions, especially in stressful times or those that may trigger past memories or experiences. DBT will guide a person on how to change the emotions they want to change and learn effective ways to work through overwhelming feelings.

- **Distress tolerance:** This ties in with the above point in that the individual learns tools to tolerate painful events and the emotions attached to those events. It also includes understanding when we can't make things better right away but don't want to make things worse by allowing emotional responses to take over.

- **Interpersonal effectiveness:** This is a difficult skill set to embrace, especially for those who have difficulty with boundaries. Under this point, the individual learns how to ask for what they want and to be okay with saying no to things they aren't comfortable with or can't handle. They learn skills that will build and maintain their self-respect so they can have healthier and more meaningful relationships with others.

- **Staying on the middle path:** This is probably the most important part of DBT. Staying in the middle means the individual learns to replace unhelpful, non-effective, and rigid thinking with more healthy and flexible ways of thinking. The key is finding the balance between acceptance and change.

In addition to these points, there are those to are also dealing with past trauma. This is another focus of the DBT process that will not only help the individual face and work through that trauma but also how not to allow that source to continue running their life.

Every one of us deserves to live as happy and healthy as possible, and DBT is a highly effective way to ensure this. The process teaches how to take the fragmented parts of ourselves and re-unite them, so we have a renewed sense of wholeness. As we'll soon see, focusing more on the things we *can* control and letting the rest go is the most empowering part of DBT. Whether the person is an individual living with mental health struggles or someone who cares for and loves them, the benefits of learning and embracing these skills will be well worth the effort put in.

CHAPTER 1

The Inside Scoop of DBT

Life doesn't make any sense without interdependence. We need each other, and the sooner we learn that, the better for us all.

–Erik Erikson

Many people who come to, or who have been referred to, a DBT program has most likely tried several treatment options already. For those who have recognized psychological or mental health conditions that aren't responding to common medicinal, basic therapy, or a combination of approaches, a more intense form of treatment may be required. In these cases, DBT has become the most successful form of therapy.

Those who have personality or mood disorders that impair their ability to function effectively, or those who get to a point where they're convinced they can't be "fixed," need a deep, inner restructuring to guide them not only to see the world differently but also on how they can maneuver within that world. This can happen by learning new skills to regulate thoughts, emotions, and reactions when in certain scenarios. But one of the most important first steps is making sure an approach is best suited to the person's symptoms and mental health goals.

In this chapter, we'll discuss the history of DBT—knowing how it came about, how it evolved, and how one person understood how crucial the mindfulness piece is in treatment. For some conditions, this was the missing element that explained why "common" paths didn't work. We'll also discuss the main focus areas of DBT and who this form of therapy would benefit the most, including the pros and cons. Finally, we'll compare and contrast DBT with other forms of therapy.

Once armed with all the right information, both the person participating in DBT as well as their loved ones will be more at ease knowing what to expect and that they're finally on the right path.

The Ins and Outs of DBT: History, Origins, and Therapeutic Goals

DBT was founded by a researcher named Marsha Linehan.

Initially, she was conducting research for severely high-risk suicidal individuals and trying to find other treatment avenues for this group of people. Combining both her personal experience from coping with severe mental health issues in her teens as well as observing that common therapies at that time weren't as successful in more severe cases, she realized the need for a different approach.

At the time, the most common therapeutic approaches were from the behavioral view or the humanistic approach, both having strong points. Behavioral therapists focus on reactions/responses to external stimuli in an individual's environment. In other words, there is a strong belief that our behavior is learned and that we can unlearn those behaviors with some guidance and re-direction. Humanists see things a bit differently. Humanistic therapists see the individual as a whole person and believe that behavior doesn't stem from stimuli or reinforcement alone. They believe that individuals need to have a balance among their mental, physical, emotional, and spiritual sides, and when one area is impaired, it causes a trickle effect on the other areas. Linehan made her own observations from these two very strong viewpoints and derived her approach of DBT.

She noted that those who were more severely affected by their suicidal thoughts didn't usually respond well to the behavioristic view of focusing specifically on redirecting cognitive thoughts.

People were often made to feel that their condition was their fault, and they simply needed to change their thought patterns in order to change their behavioral responses. It's not always as cut and dry for many people. They needed to understand the connection between thinking, feeling, and acting on those things in order to learn the most effective self-regulation skills. But there were other components she realized also needed to be considered when treating such individuals.

Understanding only the observable reactions and basing treatment on those reactions alone isn't considering deeper elements that can also impact a person's overall health. For example, those who are inundated with suicidal thoughts may be living with past trauma that has frozen them from being able to get past it. Such a person would benefit from not only understanding their reactions and behavioral responses to certain situations but also healing their emotions and memories attached to that trauma so they can continue moving forward. That's the base of mindfulness, which is what Linehan realized was missing from therapeutic approaches of that time. When personality conditions, most specifically behavioral personality disorder, were recognized, this need for a new avenue became essential.

Linehan created a new path of treatment that embraced both insight from behavioral views as well as the humanistic that became known as DBT. The main goals are guiding people to live in the moment, develop healthier ways to cope with stress, regulate their emotions, and improve their relationships with other people. So, there is still a focus on behavior, but it also involves an understanding of *why* one behaves the way they do and how to learn new skills to cope with stressors in a more effective way. This concept represents the "dialectical" part of DBT, which is the learning of skills in two opposite areas (e.g., acceptance and change).

The DBT process passes the individual through four different stages:

- **Stage one:** At this point, the person may be feeling out of control and that nothing will be able to help them. The initial focus is on stabilization as the individual may be plagued with suicidal thoughts, self-harm, and/or addiction. They are at their rock bottom and see no future for themselves. Safety and crisis intervention is the number one priority so that the person can regain some level of stability and not be in immediate danger.

- **Stage two:** In this stage, there is still concern for behavioral reactions, but the person is more stable and not in danger. Their mental health issues are still just under the surface, as well as their inability to regulate their emotions. Any sort of trauma is looked into as a source of their current mindset. The goal of this stage is to help the person face their emotional pain as it comes up, rather than burying or ignoring it.

- **Stage three:** When the person reaches this stage, the root of their struggles has been put into the light, and they learn to live the rest of their lives more productively. The focus within this stage is to become future-oriented, build self-respect, and find peace and happiness around them to encourage their positivity.

- **Stage four:** This stage isn't required for all individuals, but for some, it's a much-needed part. For those people who have been living with their pain for an extended amount of time, therapists continue working with them in solidifying life skills and attaining fulfillment through strengthening their spiritual self (however this may be seen to them).

There will be expected steps forward and back as the person is moved from one stage to the next, but the main goal is for the person not to fear what comes up in the rest of their life's journey because they'll have learned the right coping skills to regulate themselves.

How Does DBT Work?

DBT was originally developed to help those who are suicidal and, eventually, for those diagnosed with borderline personality disorder, or BPD, as suicidal thoughts or attempts is a major symptom of BDP. Today, the form of therapy is used for those with chronic or severe mental health issues who suffer from self-harm, eating disorders, PTSD, or other forms of trauma and addiction.

It is a highly intensive program requiring the person's willingness to commit to the time and effort on their part, which usually takes approximately a one-year timeframe. Some may not need the entire time, while others may find they need more. It all depends on how they progress through each stage and the individual's capacity to embrace the different components.

The basic DBT-based program focuses on five components that each has a specific function:

- **Group skills training:** This is usually carried out in a group or class format. The therapist gives tasks to help individuals learn effective and practical skills in their lives when they are distressed to replace the unhealthy and negative behaviors they usually turn to. The group meets weekly for a few hours and takes approximately 24 weeks to get through the full skills curriculum. The content is often repeated to equal the one-year program. The main skills focused on include mindfulness, distress tolerance, interpersonal effectiveness, and emotional tolerance, which are emphasized throughout the program. We'll go into further detail about these skills later on.

- **One-on-one sessions:** These are carried out weekly for about an hour or an hour-and-a-half where the individual and the therapist work through specific challenges, concerns, or events in the person's life. Because mental health issues are individual, no two people will have the exact same plan. These sessions are important as they help the person stay focused on their goals and address anything that they're struggling with to reach those goals.

- **Consultation team:** Most individuals in this form of therapy have life-threatening behaviors that can be challenging, even after successfully completing the program. Therefore, DBT therapists work with consultation teams that consist of professionals who meet regularly to be on the same page in doing their part in navigating the individual through potential stressors, helping them stay motivated, and delivering overall good therapy.

- **In-the-moment therapy:** There will be times when the

individual may become overwhelmed and feel themselves falling into crisis mode. In such moments, their therapist will coach them through the stressful event or trigger and remind them of their DBT skills. The goal here is to guide the person to turn to their learned skills and put them into practice in their day-to-day lives. Unlike other therapy programs, those in DBT will be able to access someone on their treatment team by phone for in-the-moment support. The therapist is a member of the individual's support network, which we'll discuss in a later chapter.

- **Case management strategies:** This component empowers the person to take back control of their life and self-care. The therapist guides the individual to apply learned strategies to their regular life events so that they can become their own case manager.

The end goal of these elements is to help the person learn to create future-oriented goals and build a life they feel is worth living.

What Is the DBT Skills Training Part of the Therapy Program?

These are the skills discussed above under the point on group skills training. Learning these skills seems to be what makes the program so difficult for many individuals. This is because they need to change the way they've always coped with uncomfortable thoughts and emotions to more effective and healthier ways. These are taught by guiding the individual through critical skills grouped within four different modules:

- **Mindfulness:** This is learning the importance of focusing on the events happening in the present and acknowledging their thoughts, feelings, and behaviors as they come out without trying to control them. The point is learning and embracing the fact that we have no control beyond ourselves. We can't control what others do, say, think, or feel, but we *can* control the way we respond to such things.

- **Distress tolerance:** The point of learning this skill is all about acceptance. Understanding and accepting the things we don't have control over helps strengthen problem-solving skills and improves mood. Learning how to cope effectively in a crisis and accepting a situation or person as it is, rather than obsessing with how it should be, is key. This is also the entire premise of living mindfully. Learning this skill stops impulsive or self-harming behavior, and reminds the person there are more constructive alternatives.

- **Interpersonal effectiveness:** This module emphasizes

learning the skills to have healthier relationships by practicing good self-care. This involves working the individual through any conflict, listening effectively, and clearly asking for what they need. It also includes strengthening their ability to ask for what they need and knowing it's okay to say no. In other words, it means learning to create solid boundaries while still maintaining self-respect and relationships with others.

- **Emotional regulation:** This module teaches the individual how to manage their emotions properly so they can further control their thoughts and behaviors. Basically, it helps them label their emotions but not judge them. They'll understand that different emotions shape their behavior and what may be preventing them from regulating their emotions properly. Finally, they'll learn when to avoid situations that trigger uncomfortably strong emotions and turn to events and others that boost positive emotions.

It's clear that DBT can prove to be beneficial either as an alternative path or in conjunction with other approaches. It greatly depends on the individual's overall focus, the severity of their condition, and dedication to their therapy.

Is DBT Right for Me?

This is a fair question, especially for those who've tried several other therapy avenues with little or no success. The entire reason we embrace professional help or guide our loved ones to it, is we want more than anything to live the most fulfilling, happiest life possible. It's a bit intimidating when we're told straight off the cuff that this sort of treatment is intense, requires us to put in a lot of effort, and can bring up specific memories or emotions we've tried to ignore. Knowing all of this can make us wonder if DBT is the right path, how/if it would benefit us, and what the pros and cons are.

As with any form of therapy, the person needs to have a strong willingness to give it a try. If we don't believe something will work going into it, it won't. There has to be an open-minded approach and even a glimmer of hope that it could make a difference. Even though DBT is geared specifically to those who have more serious conditions with strong suicidal and self-harm thoughts, it may be right for others in cases where

- They struggle with regulating their emotions

- Their emotions are intense or eruptive

- They struggle with anger issues

- They see the world from a black-and-white view

- Their moods are either extremely high or very low with no gray area

- They're extremely sensitive

- They feel as though their life is out of control and don't see their life in a future-oriented way

- Their social or intimate relationships are unstable and unpredictable

- They embrace a sense of hopelessness and/or emptiness

- They've had little or no success with other forms of therapy

- They often turn to maladaptive, and sometimes dangerous, ways of coping, such as substance abuse, self-harm, or high-risk behavior

The bottom line is that if an individual's emotions interfere with having healthy relationships, reaching personal or professional goals, or leaving them feeling out of control, overwhelmed, or debilitated, DBT can prove helpful. Another way a therapist can help with determining whether this form of therapy is best suited to an individual's needs is by knowing the pros and cons.

Pros:

- Most importantly, it's backed up by research, which means it's evidence based. It doesn't just help with mental health struggles and guides a person to living a more productive life. It also reduces symptoms of anxiety, depression, trauma, and stress, as well as decreases suicidal and self-harming thoughts.

- It improves mood.

- It helps to rebuild self-esteem, self-worth, and quality of life.

- Patients have access to their therapist, even during "in-the-moment" times.

- The components of the program give ways for the person to learn and practice skills in a safe environment.

- This form of therapy has been proven effective regardless of age, gender, sexual orientation, social status, or culture.

- DBT has been incorporated into other therapeutic plans for those being treated for psychosis, mania, substance use, eating disorders, and adolescent mental health struggles, and has even been helpful in creating profiles in forensic settings!

- It's one of the few forms of therapy that includes the element of mindfulness, which is a major element for those requiring help in developing a present-oriented mindset.

- It teaches individuals to embrace the gray area where things aren't always black-and-white, right-or-wrong, or all-or-nothing.

Cons:

- DBT requires *a lot* of time commitment.

- There are certain elements that a person may find so overwhelming, it can elicit fear and an unwillingness to continue.

- It requires the person to do "homework," which may not feel comfortable for some.

- The DBT program is highly structured with firm boundaries that are expected to be met. A person with certain conditions, such as BPD, may find this difficult.

- There's no formal trauma processing element in the program. This means those with a serious trauma-based condition may require the trauma to be treated simultaneously with DBT to achieve greater success.

- When considering the mindfulness element, the philosophies in healing the spiritual self may not be acceptable within certain religious values.

- Due to the intensity of certain elements of the DBT program, there's a possibility of increasing risky behavior as an individual faces certain events. Therefore, clinicians must be highly trained mental health professionals who are best prepared to foresee these situations if/when they arise.

When weighing whether or not to consider DBT, individuals who have struggled with depression, anxiety, self-destructive thoughts, and harmful behaviors come to the therapeutic table feeling they can never overcome their symptoms. The most important aspect of DBT is that it helps rewire our brains and learn new reactions to stressors and uncomfortable thoughts and emotions. For some people, it truly is the very last try finding the help they so desperately want to live the best life possible. It will be hard to put trust into yet another therapy, but the courage, effort, and determination needed to be put into DBT will be well-rewarded.

Chapter 2

A Closer Look at DBT Components

Just because no one else can heal or do your inner work for you doesn't mean you can, should, or need to do it alone.
–Lisa Olivera

For those who've been there for a loved one struggling with mental health struggles and have been alongside them witnessing one form of therapy after another not coming close to what it promised to achieve, being referred down yet another therapy path may require some solid assurance. At this stage, the person going through it, as well as the people supporting them, just want some glimmer of hope that *this time*, something will click. That's what we're hoping to do with this chapter.

In the first chapter, we went over some of the main points of what's covered in a DBT program as well as how to figure out if this path will be right for the individual. It is, after all, a minimum year-long commitment of highly interactive and very intense self-work. Although DBT has an inspirationally high success rate, it isn't an easy process at first. In fact, an individual who has worked so hard to hide their struggles may even find it on the aggressive side. For many, though, it offers that sort of gentle, loving push they need to get "unstuck" and live the very best life they were born to.

With that in mind, we're going to discuss the professional DBT team—who they each are, their focus, and what they each bring to the therapy table. It might be less intimidating to have this information before beginning so the individual goes into it understanding what's expected from them, but also what they should expect from those they're putting their trust in. The chapter focuses mostly on how these sessions are carried out through the various modules and components from both the therapist's and the individual's views.

By the end of this chapter, individuals and their loved ones should have a clearer picture of what to expect in a DBT program. Remember that every effort we put into something in life comes back to reward us 100 times over, and those are the valuable pearls of wisdom someone in the depths of mental health struggles needs to hold onto.

The Structure and Focus of the DBT Team

The DBT team isn't what may immediately come to mind. Those who've been by a loved one's side during every therapy or treatment plan have joined a team of different professionals to discuss progress and the next steps. This group of people is usually those who have worked closely with the individual, providing them with their specific area of expertise.

In the case of a young person, for example, who has a history of suicidal thoughts, self-harm, and running away, their group may include a crisis counselor, a nurse, a doctor, an occupational therapist (OT), a social worker, a psychologist, and a psychiatrist. If the youth need to have a longer stay in a hospital, there may even be members of the community, such as school contacts. Each of these professionals deals with the youth in a different capacity, and they contribute a unique view of the young person. This is how it's set in every case whether a child, youth, or adult.

What makes this process work so well is the "team approach." Initially, the idea of a treatment team was a way to make sure that the professionals involved in the therapy were following the necessary protocol and the research requirements. It evolved into a mindset that it takes an unconditionally supportive *team* to help these individuals and the value that mindset has on the individual. But the DBT team is a bit different from the traditional consultation team described above, which is seen in three core concepts:

1. **They consider themselves a community of therapists, treating a community of clients.** It may sound odd to call the people they're helping "clients," but it takes away the sterility of "patient." They give a different branch of the view that they work together to treat their clients by stating that they work as a *team* to help *all* of the people in their treatment. Each person on this team has the dedication to provide every person under their care with the best possible treatment. That means if there are times when the therapist isn't able to stay connected with an individual, or doesn't feel that client is progressing any further, another member of the team will offer insight. So, each client is seen as "our" not "my client. That is a very important aspect for a person under that team's care to feel. There's a huge sense of safety and calmness in a therapeutic group working as a unified unit, rather than as individual components.

2. **They focus on the idea of therapy for the therapist.** This point doesn't elicit a strong level of confidence initially, but it makes total sense. The idea here is that a DBT team needs to strengthen their effectiveness of their

part of the treatment given, and to be in tune with any personal obstacles that could stand in the way of the client receiving the care they need. An example would be if a provider can't progress past a specific point in the client reaching a goal, the rest of the team with brainstorm and come up with suggestions to help that provider to move the client forward. DBT providers need to accept a certain vulnerability that aren't shown in other treatment teams. This group work with individuals who are at the most severe level of emotional and behavioral turmoil, so it is imperative that DBT provider know from the get-go what their buttons are, and how to properly handle themselves when those buttons are pushed.

3. **There is a strong emphasis on dialectics.** This goes both with the approach to the DBT team as well as to their approach to therapy. As discussed in the first chapter, the entire perspective of DBT is embracing aspects from different therapeutic theories. The main idea behind dialectical thinking is that everything is made up of opposites, and in order to understand things better it's essential to understand those opposites. This is a difficult concept for many people being treated through DBT methods because they come to the table with black-and-white, right-or-wrong, and good-or-bad viewpoint. They

don't see the gray area the DBT providers do, which is why dialectics are a main ingredient in every part of the process.

These concepts are woven throughout the entire process. It's important for those in this form of therapy, and for those who love someone who is, to think of themselves as a valuable member of this team. No one person is on their own, and that's so empowering.

Expanding on the focus of the DBT team, they each bring with them a set of specific beliefs in each person they're trying to help. These aren't facts that can be proved as right or wrong, but more points the DBT providers believe in their clients/patients, so they know they're getting the best possible care suited to their individual needs:

- **Clients are doing the very best they can.** It's so easy to believe that individuals aren't trying when they keep resorting to their self-harming ways. This return to familiar, maladaptive ways of coping is frustrating for all members of the DBT team. It's important to remember that it could be one tiny thing to set the person off in that direction, even when they may seem to be having an overall good week and are progressing well. This week there's a hurdle, but next week there may not be. They are doing the best they can in that moment, and that's important to embrace.

- **Clients *want* to improve.** This is an extension on the above one. When the person isn't showing signs of improvement, it's usually because of some sort of emotional barrier, a lack of skill, overwhelming negative thoughts, or other factors that are interfering with improving the client's life. During these times, it's important to know these aren't hints that the client doesn't want to improve, but that they've been derailed for some reason. Did something happen during group? Did they have a poor sleep putting them into a negative mindset? Were they asked a question they weren't ready to face the answer to yet? There are many other factors that need to be checked into before a conclusion can be made.

- **Clients need inspiration to do better, try harder, and be guided to change.** As much as the person wants to, and can, improve, it may not show this in their current efforts. A DBT provider will be able to work with the client to see what obstacles, fears, or other barriers they have that may be standing in the way of their success. They believe in what the client can achieve and will do all they can to aspire the same in the client.

- **Clients may not have caused all their problems, but they still have to try to resolve them.** A huge part of DBT is that the client must learn to solve their own problems, even if they didn't cause them. It's part of being able to live a mindful life, and not being controlled by the past or in fear of the future. Even though the client may not have this skill, they need a supportive and understanding provider who'll work with them on the steps to do it on their own.

- **Clients need to know that although their lives may seem unbearable, they are in no way a burden.** Many of these people come from a history of therapies they weren't able to gain enough success from. They feel nothing has 'fixed' them, and all they're doing is wasting other people's time, focus, and worry. They, essentially, feel they are burdening their loved ones and supporters. Nothing is further from the truth. The person is suffering and may not be as receptive as they should be. It's the DBT provider's job to see the obstacles preventing the client from moving forward so they don't turn completely away.

- **Clients want to learn new ways to behave and respond to their different environments and the people in them.** Believe it or not, in most situations, these individuals are very aware of the face that their thoughts and inner voice trigger their behavior and responses as much as any outside trigger. The biggest challenge presented to the provider is to guide the client to more effective ways to deal with stress or fear. Providers make changes within the client's environment and help them to recognize their own needs so they can do their part to ensure they're met.

A DBT provider already believes in the person under their care, and only wants that individual to achieve every possible success. They see the person in the same light that their loved ones do—struggling, but full of potential.

A Closer Look Into the Four DBT Modules

We touched on this briefly in the first chapter more or less to introduce the program as a whole. In the following sections, we're going to take a closer look into both the modules and components of the DBT process. As discussed earlier, there are four modules in the DBT process: individual therapy, group skills training, peer consultation team meetings and intersession contact between therapist and patient. Let's go over each of these in more detail:

- **Individual Therapy:** This is the starting point for those in the program. It involves weekly one-on-one sessions between the therapist and the individual. This part of the program is highly structured with weekly "homework" and exercises to practice. The scaffold of the therapy is the same for each person but will be individualized to the person. There will be weekly discussions about goals and targets, and how these can be reached. As well, the person will engage in "internal inventory" to analyze how they did or didn't deal with specific events or experiences.

- **Group Skills Training:** This next component is an absolute requirement, even if the individual may not always have anything to contribute. These sessions are also weekly for one and a half hour to two hours, with anywhere from three to 10 people in a group. It's in this format that the four skills modules are worked through, and the length of time spent within this group depends on the amount of people in the group and their individual progression.

- **Intersession Contact:** In general terms, this is also known as telephone coaching. This can be set up differently depending on the situation. This is essentially a 24-hour accessibility to the DBT provider where the individual in therapy can call, text, email or arrange virtual meetings through Zoom or WhatsApp. Although this is an option on the table in every case, it's one that's closely monitored as it can become a platform of dependency. For example, just because the client has their DBT provider's cell phone and open connection to them, it doesn't mean they should act on every impulse to make contact. There will need to be rock solid boundaries put in place. This part of the therapy process is to support the person in the program as much as possible, but at the same time know they need to learn to turn to their support network as well as rely on the skills they're learning to guide them through triggers or stress.

- **Peer Consultation Meetings:** This involves a "meeting of the minds." Essentially, it's when the professionals involved with the individual meet on a weekly basis to discuss the details of their files. The focus at these meetings is to discuss the individual's progress in the program by reviewing what's working, what isn't, any updates or new information, breakthroughs, drawbacks, and any sort of medication changes. It's through these meetings that families and loved ones are briefed in terms of how the individual is doing in their program and if any changes need to be made.

Woven through these modules are the specific skills the individual will be learning and practicing, which we'll be going through in the next section. Although there is at least a one-year commitment expected in a DBT program, how it's structured will depend on the severity of the condition, how receptive the individual is to the program, and their age. The set-up of the program for a youth with BPD, for example, would be different from that of an adult with the same diagnosis.

A Closer Look Into the Essential DBT Skills

Although the program can help other conditions where a person is unable to cope effectively with emotional or behavioral regulation, DBT was created to help clients who struggle with BPD. DBT is intended to help those who are highly sensitive to their environment, are highly reactive to events, often become overwhelmed by their emotions and thoughts, and are difficult to calm down after an episode. Many of these clients have often experienced some form of trauma or have other undiagnosed or untreated conditions.

As discussed earlier, DBT assumes that clients are doing the best they can and that they want to get better. They'll learn that their emotions are normal and natural and that they do have control over how they respond to people or events that trigger those emotions. They'll learn new skills that they'll be guided to apply in all contexts of their lives. Clients may not have caused all their problems, but they'll learn to solve all of them anyway. The most important aspect is that they know even when there are times they go back a few steps in their treatment, it's not a "failure." Every effort put in is another tiny move toward success and happiness.

In this section, we're going to cover the DBT skills, or tools, that each person learns throughout their program. Not only do clients learn about them, but they're also given homework and opportunities to put these skills into practice. It will help families, loved ones, or other people in the individual's support network to understand these tools as well so they can remind their loved one when they seem to veer off when under stress.

Mindfulness: This is known as the backbone of DBT as there are conditions that hold a person in their past because they fear their future. It's vital that a person learns to focus on what's going on around them in a specific moment, recognize how events or people make them feel, and connect those things before reacting. The concepts of mindfulness relate to those of meditation, specifically the point of being as self-aware as possible. There are three different skill areas that together great the mindfulness mindset component:

- **Wise Mind Skills:** This is a combination of both our logical and emotional mindsets. The emotional mind keeps emotions in control, and the more logical side isn't present. A person stuck in the emotional mindset may seem out of control and often feel overwhelmed, stuck, or confused and can't find a way to move forward. The logical side is much calmer. The logical side is more rational in situations and pays more attention to the facts with little or no emotion. Normally, our decisions and actions are controlled by the logical side. A person who has learned to tap into their wise mind uses input from both emotional and logical mindsets and mixes in intuition.

- **What Mind Skills:** Mindfulness is all about living life fully, so this part of DBT is focusing on the elements that bring us to that point. This is done through three different ways:

  - **Observe** by paying attention to events, emotions, and thoughts, not avoiding painful feelings, enjoying pleasant emotions (but not to extend them past when they're felt), and being willing to experience everything with full awareness.

  - **Describe** all emotions and acknowledge thoughts, try not relating thoughts and emotions to specific events or experiences, and just make note of all that's felt or thought without judgment or labels.

  - **Participate** willingly in the event at the moment, learn not to be self-conscious, and give attention to the event at hand.

- **How Mind Skills:** This is the part of mindfulness that is difficult for some people as it requires the ability to be non-judgmental, only focusing on the moment while pushing all other distractions aside, and to focus on what we hope to come from the event. This can be difficult for a person who has been stuck in a black and white way of seeing things, which is the opposite of the entire concept of being non-judgmental, which means seeing that gray area and being okay with it. It also means judging behavior while not criticizing the self or others, and it means only focusing on what's observed. Being mindful means not being distracted by past events, obsessing about the future, and staying right in the moment we're in. In the end, it involves doing what works, and doing what needs to be done to achieve the desired outcome.

Mindfulness is certainly not an easy mindset to grasp. It takes a great deal of practice and devotion. But once it's learned, it truly does inspire every other part of DBT.

Distress Tolerance: This is another skill individuals with certain conditions learn through DBT. Generally, distress tolerance is the ability to effectively manage actual or perceived emotional stress. For those who have emotional or behavioral conditions, self-regulation is a challenge causing them to become overwhelmed more easily than most other people. Therefore, DBT providers help these individuals get through a crisis and know how to prevent one before it actually occurs or when one can't be avoided. The bottom line is learning the acceptance of reality. There are seven skills under this component that are taught:

- **ACCEPTS:** This is an acronym on helping individuals remember to get through a stressful situation one moment at a time, rather than thinking of it as a whole thing to get past. It's broken down like this:

  o **A**ctivities: This is the art of distraction by diverting attention to a task that needs to be done. This can be anything from doing a crossword, reading a chapter in a book, or getting through a short workout.

  o **C**ontributions: This is the idea of participating in an event that's beyond oneself. This can be reaching out to someone who needs help to volunteering.

  o **C**omparisons: The person would think of a time they felt different from how they feel in that moment, or they would think about how others who are at the same level of wellness they're at, or less, are coping. The whole idea behind this point is remembering there is always another person out there who may be going through something worse or is handling it in a less effective way. It's a way to shine a brighter light on the situation.

- ○ **E**motions: The individual would tap into a source that elicits emotions different from how they're feeling in a given moment. Some examples are reading an emotionally charged book, watching a show, or going to a scary movie. The whole idea is to distract current emotions, not hide from them.

- ○ **P**ush Away: The idea here is to mentally push the situation away for a while. If it's too difficult to deal with in that moment, the individual puts a mental barrier between themselves and that event, and they can come back to it later when they feel a little stronger.

- ○ **T**houghts: The idea here is to prevent thoughts from getting too powerful to shut down. This can also be thought of as positive distractions that force the person to engage their attention and focus on another activity.

- ○ **S**ensations: An occupational therapist, OT, can help with this. The idea is to use a sensory distraction different from the one eliciting the emotional reaction. Some examples are to listen to loud music, squeeze a stress ball, chew crunchy thinks like ice or granola, or even submerge in a hot or cold bath.

- **TIP:** This is another acronym that tries to change body chemistry that happens during the fight-or-flight response. The idea is to reduce the effects of an overwhelmed emotional mind when the person's thinking and behaviors are controlled by their emotions. Here's how it looks:

  o **T**ip the Temperature: Sometimes the sudden shock of cold has an instant calming effect. Splashing the face with cold water, plunging hands in a bowl of ice water, or holding a cold ice pack or cold cloth on the eyes for about ten to 30 seconds.

  o **I**ntense Exercise: This is very effective for those who have panted up emotional energy. Even engaging in intense exercise, like running, lifting, jogging, or jumping can expel enough negative energy and emotions to calm the body down.

  o **P**aced Breathing: This is another term for intentional breathing. It's used in meditation and yoga practices in order to calm the mind and body to a resting state.

- **Self-Soothing:** This involves tapping into our senses. The person should do things that feel pleasant, comforting, and provide relief from stress or pain. The point is to pass the time without making things worse. There are many ways to do this, and it's highly independent. There are those who are calmed through touch, while others find the sense of touch is enough to send them over the top. The senses are closely connected to both memory and emotional responses, so this should be trodden into carefully and with the individual's explicit comforts and triggers in mind.

- **IMPROVE:** The person uses this skill to improve the stressful moment they're presently in by replacing it with a more positive memory. The hope is that this skill will make the present moment more pleasant and easier to tolerate. The different suggestions are broken into the acronym:

  - Imagery: The person envisions a calming, beautiful scene such as mountains, a lake, a waterfall, or even a spot in their home.

  - Meaning: Finding meaning in everyday tasks or events helps to guide the person to purpose and something more positive to take their mind to.

  - Prayer: This is a very personal thing, and not every one

of us follows a specific religious denomination or even prays in the same way. The whole idea is to find strength in connecting to a higher power, however it looks to the individual.

○ **R**elaxation: The moment could be improved just by practicing calming techniques. The most effective are those mentioned earlier by easing oneself through sensory methods.

○ **O**ne: Some individuals may find this one difficult as it involves focusing on only one thing in the situation at hand. For those who find it difficult to tune things out, it can pose a challenge, but with practice it gets easier.

○ **V**acation: This gives permission to take a break from adulthood for a while. Go build a sandcastle, play with the dog, or even take a nature walk.

○ **E**ncouragement: As much encouragement, inspiration, and support the person is receiving from everyone around them, they also need to give themselves pep talks once in a while. Again, this may not be the easiest exercise initially because it involves saying positive affirmations about themselves.

• **Pro/Con:** For those who struggle with making decisions

or solving problems, this is a great tactic. It involves describing the stressful situation at hand, thinking of all of the good and bad that could result from acting on their reactions., and then having the ability to come to the best decision for themselves and those around them.

- **Problem-Solving:** This is an extension of the above skill. In this point, the individual would see the problem at hand and how it interferes with reaching their goals. The person should try thinking of a few options to choose from to move them out of their usual black-and-white line of thinking. It also involves acknowledging what the results of each option would be. From there, the person is in a good position to make the best possible decision.

- **Radical Acceptance:** This means to completely accept reality. The reality of a situation is in the mind, heart, and body. This helps the person stop fighting reality and learn to accept it.

Individuals in DBT need to be guided to remembering that there's a need to let go of any resentment or bitterness and accepting reality—however it's seen—exactly the way it is; rejecting or ignoring it doesn't change anything. Everything has a reason and a cause, and life is worth living. Most importantly, pain is a reality, and it has to be dealt with. It can be frightening, but in order to keep moving forward, painful events can't be avoided. It's part of the whole process of healing.

Emotional Regulation: This is the third set of skills taught in the DBT process. It focuses on the importance of emotions but on learning better ways to both regulate as well as control them. Many people coming into DBT struggle with their emotions, as well as leading with them as their way of responding to situations and people. The goals of this point are being able to name and understand emotions, reduce the escalation of negative emotional responses, and decrease emotional suffering. There are several skillsets under this skill category that are covered in DBT:

- **STOP:** This is an acronym focusing on learning to intervene when emotions being to rise up.

  o **S**top. When emotions feel like they're about to explode and become uncontrollable, the person is taught to just stop. They need to be reminded not to react or respond, freeze, and remind themselves that *they* are in control of their emotions.

  o **T**ake a step back. Physically stepping back isn't necessary unless it helps to regain control. The idea of this point is to take a break from the situation, take a few deep breaths, and take time to decide how to respond.

- ○ **O**bserve. While trying to get back, it's important that the individual takes a look around them to see what's going on, who's involved, and how they're behaving. The whole idea of this point is helping the individual learn that although we can't control what others do or how they act, we have power over how we respond.

- ○ **P**roceed mindfully. At this point, the person has learned the mindful mindset and what they need to do to cope effectively. Some individuals need more time in order to respond and, especially, to make the best-suited decision.

- **Opposite-Action:** This is a very important skill for those who are more reactive than most is learning to teach themselves to respond in an opposite way than is biologically set. For example, when we're tired, the normal response is to sleep. Or if we're hungry, we know to eat. DBT providers teach individuals to develop the same connection with negative emotions such as anger, fear, shame, or guilt. These sorts of emotions can become overwhelming very quickly in some conditions but learning more effective behavioral responses to them will strengthen the control they think they have.

- **ABC PLEASE:** This skill is also one that enhances what the individual will have learned in living mindfully. The whole focus here is to reduce vulnerability; in order to be in a position to help others, we need to help ourselves.

  o **A**ccumulate positive emotions by doing things that make us happy and feel good.

  o **B**uild personal mastery by doing things that hold our interest, that we're good at, and make us feel competent.

  o **C**ope ahead by rehearsing the plan of action so that we can be prepared to cope most effectively.

  o Treat **P**hysical i**l**lness and be sure to take medications as prescribed.

  o **E**at balanced meals and snacks to avoid mood swings.

  o **A**void any and all mind-altering substances that affect mood.

  o **S**leep maintenance to rest the brain and give us energy.

  o **E**xercise regularly for mind, body, and spirit.

- **Cope Ahead:** For many individuals who live with high anxiety, or more severe conditions, such as BPD or bipolar disorder, it's important that they develop the skill of planning ahead. All this means is to understand the situation they'll go into, all possible triggers involved in it, and the most effective tools to get through it. Children, youth, and young adults are more vulnerable to becoming overwhelmed as they haven't developed strong coping skills, but they will over time. Learning this valuable skill can save a great amount of emotional stress for the individual.

- **Positive Self-Talk:** If we pay close attention to our self-talk, it may be surprising to see how unkind we can be to ourselves. Negative self-talk starts in our early years when we call ourselves "stupid" for not understanding something or all of the "I cant's" that slip out. For those who don't have a positive source to tell them otherwise, we tend to buy into that negative self-talk, and it takes time to *unlearn* that line of thinking.

Interpersonal Effectiveness: This is the fourth skill set in the DBT program. The number one thing individuals need to know is that these skill sets aren't innate but *learned*. Those negative tapes we listen to can interfere with finding healthy new relationships or being strong enough to end toxic ones. The goals in this area include getting people to meet our needs, having others respect our personal goals, and ensuring others respect our established boundaries. Emotions often get in the way of building healthy relationships. Individuals learn to strengthen current relationships, build new and satisfying relationships, and end any relationships that are unhealthy or toxic. It is important for DBT patients to create and maintain balance in their relationships, and to balance change with acceptance. There are different skills and acronyms to learn that will make this easier to embrace:

- **DEARMAN:** This an acronym intended to help individuals develop more effective interpersonal communication to ensure their needs are met, and they can allow themselves to develop healthy relationships with others:

  - **D**escribe the current situation and explain what we're reacting to.

  - **E**xpress personal feelings and thoughts, and don't assume the other person should or will know.

  - **A**ssert ourselves by making it clear what we want without the assumption the other person will figure it out. It's vital to understand others can't read our minds so we need to express ourselves effectively.

  - **R**einforce the negatives and positives for having our

need met.

- o **M**indfulness keeps us focused on our current and immediate goals, needs, and wants. All this means is staying on track by not being distracted, or reiterating points that have already been made.

- o **A**ppear confident through a strong tone of voice and body language, good eye contact, and do not back down.

- o **N**egotiate when needed. The idea here is the "give to get" approach without giving at our expense. Don't be talked into something that only benefits one person, but where each side receives something positive.

- **GIVE:** This is an important skill that's particularly important for maintaining healthy relationships through solid lines of communication. It's best learned using the following acronym:

- o **G**entle: There is some wisdom in the expression, "You can catch more flies with honey than you can with vinegar." Being gentle means acting with kindness and respectfulness and avoiding any sort of conflict. Even if a conversation leans toward areas that are painful or uncomfortable, being honest and open with not wanting to engage in such subject matter is better.

o Interest: Not every subject matter will grab our full attention, but we should always listen and be engaged, without interrupting or talking over the other person.

o Validate: Validate the other person's thoughts and feelings about the situation at hand. This skill is emphasized for a DBT receiver in every aspect of their therapy, so they need to learn to do the same thing. A part of this is learning to see the other person's point of view and moving to a different area to respect their privacy.

o Easy Demeanor: This doesn't mean disregarding the level of seriousness of the situation at hand. But the person needs to learn there's no room for attitude and to respond in an appropriate way to the other person.

• FAST: The point of this acronym is important to learn in effective communication because it helps the individual maintain their self-respect. It requires them to be honest about problems without sacrificing their values.

o Fairness: They need to be fair to themselves and to the other person while respecting the feelings and needs on both sides.

- ○ **A**pologies: When an apology needs to be given, it should be done with sincerity. But there is such a thing as over apologizing or being sorry for things they don't need to be. This skill will teach individuals to tell the difference.

- ○ **S**tick to values: This is high priority because one should never sacrifice their values or morals for any reason. These should be made clear to another person and be made known it will never be tolerated for those things to be disrespected or ignored.

- ○ **T**ruth: Above all else, honesty is essential in any relationship. DBT teaches that it's never okay to lie or be lied to, so they need to be honest and never make excuses for wrong choices or decisions, and others shouldn't be allowed to be dishonest with them.

- **Creating and Setting Boundaries:** Many people who are in DBT have a history of confusion in respecting boundaries. This means either their own weren't valued or they never learned how to respect other people's boundaries. There is a lot of time spent on the learning about, creating, and enforcing personal, physical, and emotional boundaries in DBT. After all, our emotional health relates to the healthiness of our boundaries. For those who grew up in stressful, chaotic, or dysfunctional environments, learning to use boundaries can be extremely uncomfortable. That's because it threatens how we perceive ourselves, as well as our defense and survival skills. Over time, we'll learn to see ourselves as separate from others, and that healthy, clear boundaries are a good thing. Boundaries are flexible enough that we choose what's allowed near us and what needs to stay out. That's how we learn to distinguish hostility from affection, kindness, and positivity.

In this chapter, we covered how the DBT program is set up, and took a closer look into the various components and skill sets. This is an overview from both the DBT provider's perspective and what they hope to bring the individual's they care for, as well as how the program looks from the view of the person going through the process. We went through a great deal of information here, which will make the next chapter on how supporters and loved ones can help someone close to them through the DBT process in other environments of their lives.

CHAPTER 3

DBT as a Multifaceted Form of

Therapy

I am bent, but not broken. I am scarred, but not disfigured. I am sad, but not hopeless. I am tired, but not powerless. I am angry, but not bitter. I am depressed, but not giving up.
–Anonymous

As we've discussed in earlier chapters, those struggling with more severe emotionally, personality, and/or behaviorally based conditions needed a form of therapy specific to their symptoms. Such individuals need to recognize their emotions, learn to regulate them, and change their thought patterns to a more positive and logical mindset. This will help them to respond in situations and in their relationships with others in a better way. DBT, in a sense, offers such people a sense of freedom and happiness they may not have felt before. But this form of therapy helps deal with other conditions too.

In this chapter, we want to cover other ways DBT can help individuals. Although it was branched off of CBT as a much needed and highly effective way to guide those diagnosed with BPD specifically, the therapy process can also help with the residual conditions that can stem from BPD. As we'll talk about in a later chapter, these individuals need to be treated as a whole person, not just one aspect of their diagnosis. For example, a person who lives with bipolar disorder needs to be treated for both depression *and* mania, as well as any other symptoms they may show. If a person isn't treated within all of these areas, it can lead to their condition becoming worse.

For the next discussions, the focus will be on how DBT helps in other areas of mental health, such as depression, anxiety, trauma, or other conditions that may be at the base of the individual's main diagnosis. We're also going to have separate sections outlining other treatments used in conjunction with DBT, such as medicinal and electroconvulsive therapy (ECT), and the pros and cons of these.

Up to this point we've gone over a great deal of information, which may be overwhelming at first. But for those who have a loved one with a severe mental health diagnosis and want to continue being a strong member of the individual's support network, the effort put in now is invaluable to that person's future.

DBT Going Beyond Its Main Scope

The place to begin a discussion about how DBT is often considered a better-suited therapy option for certain conditions needs to start with a comparison between CBT and DBT. There are reasons that DBT was branched off from the main concepts of DBT, and this should become clearer as we go through this section.

As mentioned in an earlier chapter, CBT is a talk therapy. CBT therapists focus on talking an individual through their problems in an attempt to restructure their thoughts differently. The therapy is based on the idea that thoughts and behaviors directly influence emotions, so changing the way we think about and react to situations will make us feel better. But this approach isn't effective for treating all mental health issues. That's the main reason for the creation of DBT.

Although DBT shares many perspectives of CBT, the focus is different. A DBT therapist helps people who display extreme emotional reactions. The idea is to guide the individual to interact with their environment and the people in it in a healthier way. The question many are left with is: "With such similar names, and understanding one is a branch off of the other, are they really that different from each other? And in what cases is using one more beneficial than using the other?"

Basically, CBT is a general term for various therapies that share common features. CBT therapists rely on the talk therapy that depends on those specific features. Those include

- Treating emotional responses with the premise that thoughts control emotions and talking about them makes a person feel better.

- Limiting treatment time to learning strategies under the guidance of a therapist, then going on to apply them on their own. If/when mood doesn't improve, the individual is moved onto another form of therapy to figure out what barriers may exist that hinder effectiveness.

- This may seem like an obvious point, but because this therapy touches on deeply personal issues, it's essential for the individual in therapy to trust and feel comfortable with their therapist.

- Relying on logic and reason to help guide how the individual responds to situations rather than allowing emotions to control the reins.

- CBT therapists have a specific reason for the techniques and methods they use in each session. They allow the client's goals to decide which concepts will be most beneficial, and they tailor each session to those goals.

DBT, on the other hand, doesn't follow all of these CBT features. Since it is a branch of that therapy, DBT is tailored more towards helping people acknowledge the pain and discomfort they feel, feel safe in a given moment eliciting those discomforts, and empower them to choose healthier behaviors over the impulsive or harmful actions they normally turn to. While some emphasis is put on dealing with thoughts, DBT patients are taught to identify their triggers in their environment and match them with a more effective coping mechanism or response.

We can see how similar these forms of therapies are, but the focus of each is what makes them more effective with some conditions while not with others. A therapeutic approach to treat conditions such as depression or anxiety can elevate those who have personality disorders. CBT has been shown to help depression go into remission more than other types of therapy. It's also highly successful in treating anxiety, as it gives patients control over their recovery. Finally, it's used for people diagnosed with obsessive compulsive disorder (OCD), phobias, panic disorder, post-traumatic stress disorder (PTSD), and sleeping issues.

DBT focuses more on teaching people how to change behavioral patterns, rather than simply thinking or talking through their issues. Those in this therapy have displayed patterns of intense emotional reactions and impulsive behaviors in response to overwhelmingly unbearable feelings of pain and rejection. DBT is the most effective therapy for those who struggle with self-harm behaviors, such as cutting, eating disorders, and/or chronic suicidal ideation, and have exhausted all other paths of therapy. Those with a past of sexual trauma have also benefitted from DBT's process.

Each form of therapy also embraces different lines of theory in its approach. CBT therapists rely on talking individuals through their problems using logical and critical thinking ideals. In other words, individuals are guided to dig deep down to find the "logical explanations" for their current struggles. A DBT therapist relies more on the mindfulness practices. They guide patients to use specific techniques with the goal of being able to live with their pain in their world and accept how things *are* instead of suffering in trying to change them.

Which form of therapy is the best? Well, that depends on the underlying diagnosis because the individual needs a method that's best suited for treating it and its specific symptoms. That's why people with depression and anxiety seem to have great success with CBT, while people with BPD or chronic suicidal thoughts find DBT better. As discussed earlier, many people can have more than one diagnosis, and in such cases the use of elements from both DBT and CBT are used at the same time to manage their symptoms more effectively.

A wise thing to do, especially in the case of people who have exhausted many other forms of therapy with no helpful results, is to research and interview various therapists until there's a good fit. After all, a person wouldn't jump right in to purchase the first car that looked good, sounded right, and had great reviews/recommendations. They'd want to give the car a test drive and see how it feels themselves. It's the same thing with a therapist. We aren't going to open up to and trust our mental health to someone just because they had great success with another person. That personal connection is individual.

DBT was created directly from the theoretical base of CBT, but it's more specialized to address the needs of people with a higher sensitivity to emotional situations. DBT therapists are able to help individuals even if they haven't been diagnosed with a specific mental health condition, and it can also help with other conditions:

- **Post-traumatic Stress Disorder (PTSD):** This condition

- develops in people who have experienced some sort of trauma that has elicited extreme anxiety. For these individuals, it isn't just that they have trouble regulating their emotions, they literally re-live the initial trauma repeatedly every time they come in contact with a trigger. They also experience depression, panic attacks, and severe anxiety that put them at a higher risk for suicidal or self-harming behaviors. DBT therapists can teach these people skills to help regulate their emotional responses and reduce self-harming behaviors.

- **Depression:** Those who live with this condition experience swings in mood that are similar to BPD patients and increase their suicidal thoughts and self-harm. Research has found that DBT therapists' guidance on emotional regulation and mindfulness help individuals reduce their depression symptoms. However, more research is needed to determine if it could help prevent relapse.

- **Anxiety:** There are several forms of anxiety and varying severity, but all involve strong feelings of fear or worry that often interfere with day-to-day life. This can lead to issues at home, work, and in personal relationships. DBT therapists treating those for anxiety focus on teaching skills to cope with overwhelming feelings in order to manage their emotions more effectively. DBT can successfully reduce anxiety symptoms and learning the ability to stay in the moment (mindfulness) might also help improve symptoms.

- **Eating Disorders:** Bulimia, anorexia, and binge-eating are difficult to treat, and the reasons for such conditions developing is individual. The main goal in treating eating disorders is to connect the episode to the emotional trigger. DBT therapists can help these individuals learn to tune into and regulate their emotions as well as learn better skills to deal with stress, emotions, or triggers in their environments.

- **Substance Abuse Disorder:** For some people, reaching out for a substance to use as a crutch or escape is easier than dealing with what drives them to it. Self-medicating is a strong symptom of underlying and unresolved events or experiences or dealing with another undiagnosed mental health condition. DBT therapists can guide individuals to deal with their emotions in a healthier way, learning new adapting skills rather than turning to substances, and to take a more mindful approach to their lives. Learning to be in the moment at hand is a powerful way to re-gain control of their lives.

- **Bipolar Disorder:** People with this condition experience radical changes in mood, behaviors, and thought processes. Suicidal thoughts are also very common in people living with bipolar disorder, especially during their depressive episodes. DBT isn't the usual therapy tried initially for these individuals, but many DBT therapists have adapted DBT skills in treating them with some success. It should be noted, though, that although there are similarities between symptoms of bipolar to those of BPD, the conditions are not the same. The individual's history with therapy and treatment should be looked into carefully before attempting the DBT approach.

- **Suicidal and Self-Harming Thoughts:** These are the conditions that DBT was originally established to help treat. In helping individuals learn to accept that pain is a part of life but dealing with it better through mindfulness and solid emotional and behavioral regulation skills can lead to an overall healthier, happier, and more productive life.

This should clarify how DBT offers the tools you need to manage intense emotions and cope with stress by learning important skills such as mindfulness, emotional regulation, and distress tolerance. In other conditions extended from what it was originally created to help treat, those in DBT can learn to accept the past, embrace the present, and welcome whatever changes may come in the future.

A Special Focus on the Effectiveness of DBT in Youth

Since the development of the DBT approach, there has been a disturbing rise in the number of teens, youth, and young adults living with heavy-duty adult diagnoses. Hospitals' pediatric mental health sections, youth rehabilitation centers, and child and youth care workers have been inundated over the last few decades trying to find ways to guide these young people to a happier and healthier way of coping with their overwhelming thoughts and emotions.

In response to these findings, the DBT program has created an area of the program called DBT-A, or DBT for adolescents. This area differs from the adult approach in that there is a larger emphasis on the importance of caregiver participation. Caregivers are actively involved and trained to develop their own skill sets in order to be the strongest supporter of their youth.

The program has included a new skill module for youth called Walking the Middle Path, which we discuss in more detail in a later chapter. This added section addresses issues that specifically come up within the family dynamics that can interfere with effective treatment. This DBT-A module teaches caregivers and youth skills in dialectics, validation, and behavior change that are needed to reduce conflict. In addition, it also provides a common language for families to work through issues.

DBT for teens also considers the youth's developmental stage. For example, DBT therapists often shorten the group session's length compared to those of adults to accommodate their attention span and level of willingness to participate. As well, there is usually more hands-on approach to teaching skills. DBT therapists are trained in understanding how adolescent developmental tasks differ from those of adults and create the best treatment plan accordingly.

Teens' needs are varied, and this customized module respects that, including the youth's diagnosis and needed level of care. Although the DBT-A module teaches the same skills as in the regular program, there are specific areas in a teen's life that may need additional focus and to be carried out in different ways:

- **Outpatient:** This is the most common way to DBT therapy but can still take many variations. Some youth may not respond as well in group settings, so the skills can be taught during individual therapy. The outpatient option also provides phone coaching in addition to the group or individual therapy. With more access to technology, there are now apps or online DBT options that can be incorporated into the regular program. Outpatient therapy is suited best to youth who are struggling but are able to function, are safe enough between sessions, and don't require higher levels of care.

- **Intensive Outpatient:** This is reserved for those who require a higher level of care, at risk of hospitalization, and inpatient therapy, compared to those in regular outpatient. Usually they'll meet more often (three to five groups per week) and may be either entirely DBT-focused or a portion of their program. The idea here is that with the more frequency of groups, the youth will be able to cover skills more than once and more rapidly, and this may give them more room to review, process, and troubleshoot in group.

- **Residential/Inpatient Treatment:** In these types of programs, the youth remain on-site for the entire day. As difficult as it can be living away from home, this style of treatment offers variations and creativity for care. Depending on the length and design of their program, the youth may be exposed to the entire sequence of DBT skills during their stay. There's also more of a focus on the specific skills they'll need to be able to function outside of inpatient treatment. Individual therapy is a main component in residential treatment, so the DBT therapist are often called to influence other groups, monitor behavior management, and interact with staff. Depending on the youth's situation, inpatient treatment often focuses more on distress tolerance and emotion regulation skills, which are vital to move towards outpatient treatment when the youth is discharged from the hospital.

- **Cognitive Impairment:** DBT-A has been adapted to adjust to treat a teen's cognitive level by simplifying the language and treatment design. Adaptations include easier-to-understand terms, more visuals, and more enticing worksheets. Group structure is also modified to accommodate different learning styles.

- **Schools:** Just as adults need to incorporate their DBT skills into their work environments, youth need to do the same in their school environments. Some schools offer DBT programs as classes or groups, called DBT STEPS-A. This is a non-clinical application where any student could benefit from learning the DBT skills even if they don't necessarily have any mental health diagnosis. The school program is entirely skills-based and eliminates the other components of the usual DBT program. Although it's administered by a non-clinician, some schools now have therapists as a part of the school team and may offer the DBT program that looks similar to the outpatient methods.

There are many DBT techniques focusing on the needs of teens that may vary from one format of the program to another, but there are several tools that are tapped into. Techniques seen in adolescent programs are a mix of core DBT skills and techniques considered important to teens. Several of these we've tapped into in previous chapters, but they are pointed out here as they are tweaked to be more easily embraced by youth. Some of these include

- **Mindfulness:** Mindfulness, as discussed earlier, is a core component of any DBT program that teaches people to be present and aware in the moment. This skill allows a teen to tolerate more and be able to use their tools to make necessary changes.

- **Radical Self-Acceptance:** This mindset is discussed in length in a later chapter. It's basically an extension of mindfulness that teaches youth to fully accept what is, or has happened, in their life. Radical does not mean being okay with any situation, but it frees one from fighting reality.

- **Walking the Middle Path:** This is a component added

to the regular DBT program focused on helping out with common teen issues. The emphasized techniques include the last three points below.

- **Dialectics:** It is the focus of recognizing and honoring two different sides of any conflict to find the common ground. For example, someone can be doing the best they can and yet feel they can do better.

- **Validation:** This is the recognition that both someone else's experience and our own experience are equally important. Even when each person disagrees, validation focuses on taking responsibility of actions, feelings, and thoughts.

- **Behavior Change:** This is a collection of techniques that helps to motivate, create, and maintain desirable changes in personal behavior.

Caregivers who may be looking for additional ideas to put the DBT-A skills into practice at home, there are a couple of paths to try out as well as several resources to tap into.

First, when loved ones may sense a meltdown in process, slowing things down and listening to what their teen is saying, doing, or feeling is the first step. It's important to release all of our own opinions or feelings and try looking at the situation at hand through the teen's eyes and experiences. Even if we don't agree with what they're saying, it's important to find something understandable and relate to it. This lets a teen know we understand them and that we're willing to listen more.

The key is starting with validating their thoughts and feelings respectively so that we help them avoid the slip into black-and-white thinking and keeping them in the present to see they're strong enough to get through any form of conflict. Even if we aren't sure what to say, just asking more questions and interest in their view is incredibly validating.

Another tactic to practice is accumulating positive experiences. When things are difficult, especially for youths who are stuck in an all-or-nothing mindset, it's easier to focus on the negatives in a situation. They have a tendency to put their energy towards fixing what isn't working, rather than seeing positive ways to resolve issues at hand. But we all need positive experiences to balance the negative. An effective distraction tactic to change this is to set aside time for activities they enjoy or that we can join in with them on.

The positive experiences should become the orbs of good energy they turn to free from consequences for their negative behavior. By putting this into practice, the youth won't lose the balance they get from those positive experiences. A note of caution here is to make sure the chosen activities aren't validating any of their usual self-harming methods. The key is to distract them away from those methods and guide them to healthier more effective ones.

We'll be discussing further ways to incorporate the DBT skills into everyday environments. Still, youth need a wider variety of resources they can reach out to when they feel they need additional support. One teen may thrive in a group setting while another feels better in a one-on-one setting. Either way, these are a few suggestions caregivers can keep within reach for themselves, or to have handy when their youth is having a tough time:

- **TeenCouseling.com:** There may be the rare occasion where the youth's usual DBT therapist isn't immediately available when they face some sort of conflict. This online resource consists of over 13,000 licensed DBT therapists who provide convenient and affordable online therapy as well as parent coaching.

- **Online-Therapy.com:** Therapists working on this site help loved ones relate and communicate better with their teenagers. There are even yoga videos for caregivers who want ways to emit calmness for themselves and for their teens.

- **Headspace:** The focus of this website is on meditation which helps both teens and caregivers deal more effectively with stress and anxiety. As discussed throughout the previous chapters, both mindfulness and meditation can change lives in countless ways.

- **Choosing Therapy's Directory:** This is an invaluable resource to help caregivers find the best-suited therapist who can work most effectively with our specific family dynamics. Caregivers can search for a therapist by specialty, availability, insurance coverage, and affordability. Therapist profiles and introductory videos provide insight into the therapist's personality so caregivers and youth can find the right fit.

These are only a few top resources, but every city should have different forms of drop-in sessions, crisis lines, and other ways a youth can reach out even if their usual support network isn't right with them. No youth should feel they are on their own to deal with big situations that trigger even bigger emotional reactions. When they feel they're supported and understood, no matter where they are in a given moment, they'll embrace that strength to self-advocate down the road.

In the next chapter, the discussion will focus on how supporters can be a strong part of the DBT team. Family and loved ones can make a huge impact on the individual's success, and also be able to offer the person the most effective and well-informed support they can. We'll have advice, tips, and even exercises family and loved ones can do with the individual outside of the therapeutic setting.

CHAPTER 4

Supporting a Loved One in DBT

You are not alone. You are seen. I am with you. So, you are not alone.

–Shona Rhimes

There are other members of the DBT team who also need to learn how they fit into the DBT treatment process: family and other close supporters. Those who've been by the individual's side from the get-go need to be brought into the therapeutic circle and learn the skills they need to help their loved one.

An important branch of DBT focuses on the importance of teaching family and loving friends or partners the effective skills they need to help their loved one cope effectively in their environment when they aren't in their therapeutic setting. The main goal in teaching DBT skills to those closest to the individual in therapy is to ensure they are *effectively helping* and *not enabling*, because there's a huge difference.

When helping a person, we're supporting them as they try to move through a tough time. We're there to lean on, to vent to, or to just offer a shoulder to release their emotions so they can face whatever they need to. The entire goal is not doing things for the person but being there as they move forward. When we enable a person, however, it's the exact opposite. Rather than giving the person strength to take responsibility for and face adversity, we're taking that responsibility away by taking it upon ourselves. In the end, the latter isn't helping because the person depends on others to take care of things for them, especially when it elicits discomfort or stress.

This chapter's discussions will focus on how family, close friends, or supportive partners can actively participate in their loved one's therapy. DBT's main premises and goals involve not only helping an individual become happier and healthier, but also includes learning more effective ways of strengthening their personal and professional relationships. That means that if the person in therapy is learning skills to become a well-functioning individual, then those sharing their environment should also be learning better skills to interact with, support, and guide them to achieving those goals.

We're going to go deeper into the discussion of being more of a supporter than an enabler and how to understand the difference. Even when we believe our actions are helping, they may inadvertently be hindering. One of the main components of DBT is showing loved ones how to offer their support in the ways the individual needs them. Family and other loving supporters' involvement in the DBT program is essential to making a true difference. We'll be sharing some DBT exercises to use at home that may prove useful.

DBT is often felt as the "last resort" for those who have severe mental health diagnoses such as BPD. This doesn't imply there's no hope, but it really is where therapists turn when all other avenues of treatment and therapy have not proven successful. There are many individuals who enter this program with that realization close to the surface, leaving them with an already existing sense that nothing will work. We're going to end this chapter by offering some suggestions for when the individual either resists continuing with treatment or hits a wall of resistance believing there's no hope for them.

One of the most painful things for those who love a person with a severe mental health condition isn't the fact they have a diagnosis. That's usually a relief because then there's finally something that can be researched, learned about, and understood. What's heartbreaking is watching their loved one get to a point where they believe wholeheartedly there's no hope for them. That's what DBT can do for loved ones. It instills that hope in them so that they can, in turn, strengthen that hope in their loved one.

It will happen.

Supporting Without Enabling

When someone we love is suffering, all we want to do is be there for them in any way we can. That's a natural, protective response. Being there is so important, and they appreciate it even when they may not seem like they do. But there's a fine line between *helping* and *enabling*, which we touched on in the opening discussion.

What happens with enabling is that we're inadvertently creating a codependent relationship. Because we're taking the responsibility away from someone who should be learning how to do it on their own, we're creating a very unhealthy place where we become over-responsible. They stop trying to do what they need to because they've gotten used to us taking care of them. In other words, they aren't going to make the effort in their own treatment after they've been allowed to avoid anything that makes them feel uncomfortable. Some examples include

- Making excuses for their behavior

- Lending them money

- Cleaning up after them

- Paying their bills or debts

- Providing transportation or a place to stay

- Generally taking care of them by doing their laundry, cleaning their dishes, or making them meals

- Pretending everything is okay when it isn't

- Making excuses for their reactions, lies, or other bad behavior so others don't think badly about them

- Saying you're not going to take care of them or do the above things, but you do it anyway

If dealing with a youth or young adult under your care, these things would be basic needs. At the same time, the individual still needs to learn personal responsibility and respect of others. Many of the above things can actually be helping, but it turns into enabling when the tasks are done repeatedly, become more of an inconvenience or hardship, their needs are a result of untreated addiction or mental illness, there continues to be irresponsible behavior, or the individual refuses to fulfill their adult roles. In any of these scenarios, we aren't helping the way we mean to.

Guilt is one of the main reasons that enabling creeps in. There are other reasons some of us tend to move into that role, such as

- Being concerned that our loved one may physically hurt themself or others, especially if this has been a pattern in the past

- Worrying that they'll get into trouble if left to their own devices, especially if they have a history of high-risk behavior

- Avoiding conflict, especially if it has been a concern in the past

- Not having to set strong boundaries, and they don't understand how to create or respect them

- Being fearful our loved one will become aggressive, run away, or commit suicide, especially if they have a history of suicidal thoughts or attempts

- Wanting to help, but feeling an overwhelming sense of guilt with having to say no

So, how do we stop enabling and begin truly helping? It's hard not to cross that fine line because for most of us, our intentions are good, and we truly are acting out of concern. Here are four things to keep in our line of vision before we go down the slippery slope of enabling:

1. **Accept we can't fix things.** The word "fix" isn't favored in the treatment process of those living with mental health struggles. We don't fix people; we help them heal and live the most productive lives they can. That being said, enabling is really just a form of trying to control a situation (or person) that's uncontrollable. It hurts to watch a loved one make poor choices, participate in risky behavior, or self-harm. The tough reality is that we don't have the power to orchestrate these things. Nothing we do or say or how far we stick our necks out for them will prevent them from doing what they do. One important point the DBT therapist will open the family's or supporters' eyes to is that we didn't cause our loved one's mental health struggles, and we aren't able to handle their condition ourselves. We can't control their thoughts or behaviors, but we do have control over how we respond to them. In DBT, realization is known as *detaching*. This is a skill DBT

therapists teach family members and supporters to remove their sense of responsibility for the irresponsible loved one and to learn to focus more on their own needs. The act of detaching also helps us remove the guilt we feel for our loved one's condition and our blame for what they're going through.

2. **Break through denial.** As touched on in the last point, denial is pretty tricky. It gives us a very different perspective of what's really happening so we can justify our enabling behavior. To make it clear, we aren't in denial of our loved one's mental health condition. What we're in denial of is seeing that our "help" is hindering our loved one's progress by not letting them take onus for their choices, actions, and behavior. The DBT therapist will help supporters work through their denial and learn the best ways of effectively helping their loved ones.

3. **Break down the shame.** This is another component of enabling, and it comes from different sources. There could be those wondering why we didn't do more or why we're doing too much now. Others may question how our loved one even got to where they are, which solidifies our shame and blame that their condition is our fault. The truth is that it's always easier for those who aren't an active part of what's going on with our loved one or deal with it

on a day-to-day basis, to form an opinion. But we need to get over that shame before we can embrace better ways of helping our loved one and before we're able to support them as they learn their own skills from their DBT therapist to do things on their own.

4. **Learn to manage our own stress and worry.** At the core of enabling, we're really trying to protect our loved one from suffering anymore. It can be terrifying watching as they aren't able to control themselves and can't seem to manage simple tasks or situations. We inadvertently enable them not just to take away some of that excessive stress and anxiety, but also to ease our own worry and stress when we don't step in.

As a strong loving supporter, it's vital that you stop doing things for your loved one. You need to accept that it isn't helping them to take their discomfort away. The DBT therapy process is very strong on teaching those who love an individual with a severe mental health condition how to be an effective part of the DBT team. As we'll discuss in the next section, family and close friends' involvement in the DBT program make a huge difference in the individual's success.

Family Involvement in DBT Is Essential

As discussed, DBT's focus is all about change, including in

emotions, behavior, and ways of thinking. The backbone of DBT is learning how to transform a person's *life-interrupting* thoughts, emotions, and actions to *life-affirming* thoughts, emotions, and actions. Family and loving supporters are main contributors to this process.

One of the most important elements in the DBT program is helping those in the program change their life-interrupting behavior into more effective ways of living. Much of the inspiration to make those changes is the affirmation individuals feel from their family and loved ones and that unconditional love and support is an essential component in the whole process. Why? Because those groups of people have a major impact on the individual's development.

Although there is more emphasis on family involvement when the person is a child or youth, the family piece is just as important in adulthood. They provide the background on things such as attitude, opinions, choices, and behavior. For changes the individual is making, and in order for their progress to continue, family members and supportive loved ones need to make changes too. Any efforts made on the individual's part will slowly dissipate if they re-enter the exact same situation they left before beginning treatment. But how does family and loved ones' involvement in DBT make a difference?

DBT taps into the main ideas found in all mindfulness practices derived from Zen Buddhism. We'll go into a deeper discussion on these practices in a later chapter, but for now we'll focus on the basic ideas, such as

- **Accepting** the world around us as it is, non-judgmentally, in the here and now, and without trying to change it

- **Understanding** that there is more than one way to view a situation and different ways to solve a problem

- **Validating** everyone else's individual perceptions; each of us experience a situation differently from our own set of circumstances

- **Validating** our own perceptions and experiences of a specific situation that comes from our own set of circumstances

- **Believing** that change happens when guided by mindful thought. Through the above point, we have the power to change how we react both internally (thoughts and feelings) and externally (words and behavior) to our situation and circumstances.

Those entering DBT are set in black-and-white or all-or-nothing line of thinking. DBT therapists guide them to see the gray area in the middle of those two extremes because that's where positive change exists. Family and loving supporters are learning similar ways to help their loved one move forward toward a mutually beneficial solution.

Our loved ones in DBT will be guided to face this perspective every day, so they're challenged to open their minds to new possibilities and new ways of thinking and behaving. Family and loving supporters are expected to do the same things and are also challenged to let go and to open themselves to new ideas.

The dialectic component of DBT is the premise of coming to the truth by seeing the two opposing viewpoints of acceptance and change. The process of DBT is that it helps us weed out falsehoods, clarifies our negative perceptions, and encourages us to live a more productive and happier life. Family and loving supporters learn tools to break away from their usual patterns of thought and behavior that have not been as productive as they believed. By embracing the guidance of the DBT therapist, family and loving supporters learn how to strengthen the balance back to the family.

Three ways that family and loving supporters' involvement make a huge difference in the DBT program include

- **A new communication method.** As our loved one goes through the DBT program, they'll be learning new skills to communicate and function in their world better, and the same will happen for those of us to have relationships with them. We'll learn a new vocabulary, which includes their diagnosis and how it affects them. The most important part will be developing a working knowledge of DBT. It makes a big difference when we not only understand what the therapy is, but also what sessions are like, what the goals are, and what each person's role is. Finally, we learn how DBT helps our loved ones change their all-or-nothing thinking to a much more balanced approach, and we'll play a role in each step.

- **Tools to use at home.** A major part of DBT is that those supporting the person in therapy are also continuing the process in their home environment. After all, if the person is thriving at therapy sessions but is not given the same encouragement or support to put those skills into practice within their other environments, they won't achieve the same success. That means that we need to learn the same skills and practice them with our loved ones.

- **Helping to promote communication and understanding.** As we've discussed, one of the main focuses of DBT is developing stronger interpersonal effectiveness. This means communicating in a way that promotes solid understanding between two people. When we're finally able to interact with our loved ones in a way we never were able to before entering DBT, it elicits a deeper relationship with them.

A DBT therapist isn't telling us how the best way is to interact with our loved ones. Their intent is to help both loving supporters and their loved ones to be on the same page. When this happens, it is much easier for the DBT skills to be set in motion most effectively.

For these reasons, it's clear how family and loving supporters' involvement is key. Not only does DBT give our loved one's space to learn and develop new skills, but it also teaches us how to guide them through their life events. Essentially, we're giving them as many opportunities as they need to practice what they're learning.

Top DBT Skills to Use at Home

The beauty of DBT is that the skills taught can be used in any area of the individual's life. Once the skills are learned, the person just needs to remember to put them into motion when the opportunity presents itself. Where they'd explode or meltdown from an uncomfortable trigger response to situations in the past, they'll now be able to recognize what's happening both inside and around them in order to cope more effectively.

There are so many useful skills our loved one is learning at DBT, but the top skills to practice at home include

- **Distress Tolerance With TIPP**: The focus here isn't to completely get rid of what's stressing the person, but to reduce their stress level enough so that a task seems more doable. TIPP is an acronym for times when emotions are running high, making it more difficult to process what's in front of us. TIPP stands for

  - Temperature: Use something cold to decrease their heart rate by splashing cold water on their face, putting a cool cloth on their head, getting them to hold an ice cube, or having them take a cool bath or shower.

  - Intense Exercise: We've suggested this in an earlier chapter. There are times when relaxation exercises work best, while other times it's better to redirect anxiety or stress by moving the body. That can be seen as going for a jog, doing laps in a pool, running on a treadmill, doing aerobics, or throwing a few punches at a punching bag. The motion of exertive exercise can be enough to help one re-group and to go back to a stressful task more effectively.

  - Paced Breathing: This is an essential part of some of the holistic approaches we'll be covering in an upcoming chapter. The idea is to inhale and exhale slowly and deliberately for a few minutes to reduce high emotional responses.

o Progressive Muscle Relaxation: This is another approach to calming the body down. The person starts at the top of the head, then gradually moves down to the toes until the whole body is in a state of relaxation.

- **Distress Tolerance:** This involves accepting the reality of a given situation and getting through all intense emotions triggered by it in the most effective way. Even after learning all the DBT skills, it can still be difficult to be confident in accepting what we can't change, more so for a person who is easily overwhelmed. But remembering their distress tolerance skills can be used to accept those unchangeable things by knowing that they still have other options. As the DBT therapist will emphasize, your loved one can accept things as they are, find another way to solve their problem, work through how they feel about their problem, or just be miserable in their situation and make things worse. These are all choices and thinking through them encourages doing a self-check to assess the problem so the individual can determine what they *can* do about it.

- **Emotional Reliance by Tapping into PLEASE:** Remembering the discussion back in chapter two, we covered an approach using the acronym PLEASE. These are the reminders of the various ways we need to practice good self-care in order to function healthier in our world. It involves accepting personal mental condition, eating balanced, avoiding any form of self-medicating, getting proper sleep, and getting some physical exercise every day. PLEASE is a way to explore whether what they feel in any given moment is anxiety, stress, overwhelm, sadness, anger, or whatever is rising to the surface. This recognition will guide them to put their emotional regulation skills into play.

- **Staying in the Middle Lane:** This means acknowledging the dialectic part of DBT, which is embracing the present as it is but also having the willingness of embrace change. The latter can be a hugely anxiety-triggering aspect for many of those living with mental health conditions. By understanding dialectics, such individuals will see that there is more than one way to solve a problem in any situation, that two things that may seem completely opposite can both be true, and the one constant thing is change. The idea is to focus completely on the conversation at hand in the moment with no past or future concerns impeding on the end goal.

- **Strong Sense of Mindfulness:** This is probably the most important component of DBT, and there are many different ways to put this skill into practice. In chapter two, we also discussed the HOW (observe, describe, participate) and WHY (don't judge, stay focused, do what works) skills. These are both ways to stay in the present moment, and to focus on what is controllable before carrying through with any course of action. This is a difficult skill set to learn, especially for those who are stuck in the black-and-white thinking mindset. But over time, and with enough opportunities to practice, it can become second nature.

These are a few of the many DBT skills that can and should be practiced often at home and in other areas of the individual's life. If these aren't as effective at home, tap into the DBT therapist's expertise, and work with them to find ones that may work better.

What to Do When a Loved One Doesn't Want Help

For those who have been closest to a loved one who has struggled with severe mental health issues, you are more than familiar with the fact that you can only do so much to help those who absolutely refuse to accept it. Standing by and watching them suffer is hard. When we've tried everything, we can and exhausted every possible avenue, it's frustrating, exhausting, scary, and out of our control. But the more we push our loved one, the more likely they'll withdraw or push us completely away. Where does that leave us?

The number one thing is to never give up trying. Even though we may think that's what they want, they really don't. Here are a few things to consider when a loved one doesn't want our help:

- **Listen with your ears and heart wide open.** When you feel like you're up against the wall, even if you thought they were finally on the right track, listen to them and validate their feelings. Maybe there's some sort of trigger you didn't know about that's putting up an invisible barrier. Ask what's going on and reflect on what they share.

- **Ask questions.** In order to find out what they want, it never hurts to ask. Even if they don't completely open up initially, at least you're showing that you're willing to understand. Find ways to support them in reaching their goals in a way that works for them. You can even ask how they feel about what they want you to do to guide them to reach those goals.

- **Don't try fixing things and give advice only if they ask for it.** The best time for you to give your opinion or advice is when it's asked for. If your loved one hasn't asked, simply give unconditional love and support. When you give them the time and space to feel heard, it reduces their defenses and they'll be more open to a conversation.

- **Work through options together.** If your loved one says straight up that they don't want to try something, just ask them their reasons without forcing anything. By showing them you care about what *they* want to do and what their goals are for an outcome, you can figure out a mutually beneficial way to make those outcomes happen.

- **Supporters need support too.** You can't even think about helping others unless you're doing okay and are healthy. How can you give your wholehearted support when you're tired, run-down, and frustrated? Aside from the DBT therapist, it's important to find others who are in similar supportive and care-giving roles you can vent to. It's a relief to have others in your corner who are on your side and refresh your focus.

An important point to remember is that when we force others to do things, even if it may be in their best interest, it can result in resentment. But, if we allow our loved one to make their own choices, or at the very least have guidance in making good choices for themselves, it leads to a stronger sense of having control over some part of their life. Not feeling as though they have any control in most other areas, can be a source of inspiration.

It should be said that there are certain scenarios when a person may not have the ability to make good decisions about their care. In situations where they are in danger to themselves or others, intervention is needed. But in most others, involving them can be enough to break through the wall of resistance to seek help.

Chapter 5

Advocating for Loved Ones in

DBT

Anything that's human is mentionable, and anything that is
mentionable can be more manageable. When we can talk
about our feelings, they become less overwhelming, less
upsetting, and less scary.

–Fred Rogers

Now that we have discussed ways to be the strongest supporting ally along a loved one's path with DBT, we're going to talk about ways to carry forward that information to also become their strongest advocate. They're learning skills in DBT that will enable them to advocate for themselves. That's the entire point of the program. There are ways we can advocate for our loved ones too. Whether that's seen as joining a local community family support group or helping to raise awareness not only for

DBT but also for the diagnosis our loved one is learning to cope with more effectively, every effort means the world to another person in therapy.

This chapter's focus is discussing different ways we can advocate for our loved ones in treatment. We're off to an incredible start by learning DBT skills with them and understanding everything we can about their condition. After all, if we understand the base of where their behavior and reactions come from, we'll also understand why they need to embrace the DBT skills to reduce potential emotional explosions. They are already learning strong skills for self-empowerment and self-advocacy with their DBT therapist, and so we'll be able to better support their efforts.

Many of us may get nervous without we can support our loved ones once they've completed their DBT program. The good news is that just because they've mastered the DBT skills, the therapy doors won't be slammed shut and locked behind them. The beautiful thing about this form of therapy is that there will be ongoing support and guidance during any moments of self-doubt or stumbling backward. These aren't signs of failure, and more common than we think. That's why we'll be discussing ways our loved ones can build the life they see worth living after DBT. We'll go over the DEAR MAN skill, strategies to accept reality, and a few reminders of the importance of mindfulness in their everyday life.

By the end of the chapter, not only will we have the tools to find acceptance and understanding for our loved ones, but we'll also have solid exercises to put into practice so they can be their own strongest voice.

Self-Empowerment and Self-Advocacy in DBT Treatment

The number one thing any of us should know about being a strong advocate is a willingness to be a strong voice, to be assertive, and to know your loved one's rights as well as your own. Any one of us can go out there and raise our fists in the air for support, but there's a way to do it that builds bridges with professionals and unites all of those in therapy rather than tearing those bridges down.

An important point to remember is that the healthcare system has many gaps, limitations, and a lot of red tape. It can be hard for family and loving supporters to navigate through it all to ensure our vital wisdom and perspective are heard. With the right knowledge and guidance, we can make a difference in our loved one's care. Family and loving supporters have been there from the very beginning with our loved ones so our voices should be included in all aspects of their therapy.

A phenomenal component of DBT is that they consider those closest to the individual in care to be a valued resource of what has worked and what hasn't, and we are included as our loved ones progress through each step of their DBT program. That's what gives us the knowledge to advocate for our loved ones in terms of their diagnosis, their care, and how they're treated in the community. Other people's stigmas and misunderstanding of mental health is a huge part of why our loved ones often feel like an outsider, even after they've worked hard to learn skills not to feel that way. They need to feel comfortable with the fact that they have a strong supportive team behind them to draw strength from, and to be their voice when their own may not be loud enough at times. *That's* what we do through advocacy. Not only do we support their voice, but we also help to build their confidence to advocate for themselves.

When supporting them in that way, though, we need to make sure we truly are helping our loved ones and not inadvertently hindering their own efforts of self-empowerment and self-advocacy. After all, there will be times when we aren't right there with them, and they have to rely on their own skills. Here are a few things to keep in mind about standing up for our loved ones:

- **Focus on making a difference.** The person in care is doing all of the hard work. By sticking with their DBT program, they're doing everything they can to become an active part of their world with the end goal of finally being happy in that world. Although we're also learning skills to help us understand and be there for them more effectively, we have no control over what works, what doesn't, or even if it will. Through advocating for their diagnosis as well as their therapy, it gives us a positive place to put our worries, concerns, and energies. We feel that in this one area, we are doing something positive by raising awareness for mental health, opening more doors for those not knowing where to turn, and to clear the path for others going through the same struggles. In a sense, we're not only standing up for our loved one, but also empowering others to do the same for someone in their own lives who may be struggling.

- **There should be a sense of a united front.** When there's a united voice on an individual's care between those closest to them and the professionals trying to help them, it solidifies the chances of success for the person in care. When they feel that their DBT team is solid, they'll be more inspired to see things through.

- **Understand the DBT professional standards.**
Understanding DBT and how it works is one thing but
having a deep understanding about the professionals on
the team is even better. As we discussed in chapter two,
the greater our understanding of each person's role on the
team, the better it will be in the long run for the person in
care. Research the professional associations and
understand what's expected from them as DBT team
members, and how we fit within those expectations.
Considering the level at which DBT therapists work with
individuals, they're expected to adhere to high standards
of care, respect, and empathy. Loved ones have every
right to ensure that their loved one in care is receiving
these high standards, and to know who to go to when they
aren't.

- **Ensure we're included as a DBT member.** We've gone
over this point several times, but it needs to be re-stated.
In situations where DBT may be the "last hope", we
shouldn't be shy about making sure everything that can
possibly be done, is. We have the right to shop around,
get second opinions, and even submit complaints about a
DBT member's lack of good care. These are all ways to
advocate for our loved ones in care. The number one
question we shouldn't be afraid to ask before agreeing to

anything is how family and close supporters' roles are considered in the entire process. There are some agencies or hospital programs that may not have the same openness of family involvement so gather all the information before making the choice best suited for our loved one.

- **Be in control of emotions.** If the path to getting into a DBT program has been a long and turbulent one, there may be some negative emotional baggage with us. It's natural when we've been there with our loved on in care as they've struggled through one form of therapy after another with no real success. It's vital that we do not allow negative emotions to cloud any hope and to stay as calm and collected as possible. There may be times when things may not progress as quickly as we hoped, or we don't receive immediate responses to our inquiries. We can't give up or react negatively. Always show DBT team members that you think rationally and avoid blaming and criticizing the team so that you're taken seriously. We want to be an asset to the team, not seen as a deterrent for the loved one in care. That means sticking with what we want in terms of goals for our loved one in care while eliciting positive energy at all times.

To advocate in the strongest way, we need to be learners and teachers. That means showing interest in wanting to understand all aspects of the DBT program and those on the team, and a desire to share their visions of therapy with others. We need to remember that we get the quality of treatment for our loved ones that we insist upon, with no exceptions. In the end, when our loved one knows they're being supported at this level, they'll feel better about standing up for their care and for themselves in general.

Self-Empowerment and Self-Advocacy for Mental Health Care

We as loving supporters speak out on behalf of our loved ones in care. How can we empower them to speak on their own behalf? This is the base of *self-advocacy*, and it gives our loved ones a sense of feeling empowered. It means the person is representing themselves or their interests. It means being strong enough to stand up for what we believe in and having our needs respected by those around us. It's one of the strongest skills DBT therapists teach people in their care, and for essential reasons.

DBT therapists work with people in their care to learn to feel more autonomy and control in their lives. They want our loved ones to feel independent not only in their care, but in their overall happiness and life in general. Learning these skills increases self-esteem, self-confidence, and, most importantly, elicits a sense of competence and their ability to cope with life transitions and sudden changes they face.

As in all areas of DBT, treatment is done *with* the person and not *to* them, which is much different than is seen in other areas of the mental health field. When treatment is being done *to* a person in care, their values, needs, wants, and goals aren't taken into consideration. Decisions about their life are being made *for* them, which isn't really inspiring any sense of self-empowerment. DBT therapists take a different approach.

They work *with* people in their care and include them in their own treatment. They're working alongside with people in their care in terms of what they want and need, just as those of us have been focused on the entire time. DBT therapists, as we do, take our loved ones' values, hopes, dreams, and needs to heart and consider them vital to their overall care. After all, our loved ones' mental health wellness is *theirs*, and that's exactly how the DBT team sees the situation too. We are all a part of the DBT team made up of family, loving partners, friends, and treatment providers who all want to be a part of the therapy journey.

In advocating for our loved one in care, we're being a part of that united voice we discussed earlier. But it also includes involving the person in advocating for themselves, and here are a few valuable ways we can help with this goal:

- **Ask questions.** The steppingstones of teaching our loved one how to advocate for themselves is not to be afraid of asking questions about anything they're unsure of. The biggest piece to being able to confidently stand up for ourselves is to have all the information we need in order to do that. Which means, even when their DBT therapist may be pushing them a bit too hard on days they aren't feeling strong enough to handle the emotions, they should feel they can express that. Encourage them to reach out, honestly say when they're struggling, and ask for ways to work through things when they aren't sure. That's the core of DBT!

- **Be in tune with personal wants and needs.** A person struggling with certain mental health conditions may not be in touch with their wants or needs or may not even know what they are. Before they can stand up for those things, they need to learn what they are. When our loved one struggles with this, they should know it's okay to reach out to their DBT therapist who'll be able to help those wants and needs out.

- **Fact check.** Until the person was in their DBT program, they may not have fully understood their diagnosis. Once they're brave enough to ask questions about their condition, they'll start to the connect between their symptoms and what they're doing in DBT. Knowledge is power, especially for those in therapy.

- **Repetition creates permanency.** This emphasizes an important point. There isn't a thing called "perfection" in the therapy process. Striving for perfection is what has brought many individuals into the therapy journey in the first place, so it isn't a word that's used in the process. But the process of practicing DBT skills until they become second nature, or "permanent," is a goal.

- **Become a master of something.** A way to build self-empowerment is by encouraging our loved one to learn something that makes them feel confident and competent. This could look like learning and mastering a new ability or fine-tuning one they already have. It should be a goal to take on a challenge every day that elicits these feelings and gives them a sense of control over their own happiness and the direction their life goes in.

Teaching self-empowerment and how to be their own advocate is probably the greatest gifts we can give our loved ones in care. As they move through their DBT program, they'll have days where they'll be facing things they haven't before. On those days, it's even more important for them to feel there is hope and that they do have control over the negatives they may face. When they see those around them supporting them and being a voice on the days when they don't feel strong enough to do it themselves, that's inspiring.

Helping a Loved One Build a Life Worth Living Through DBT

When an individual starts off in DBT, they're faced with a rather daunting question: What will make *your* life worth living? For those coming to the DBT table for the first time, they may have no idea how to process the question. They're usually at the end of their rope, perhaps after trying almost every other path, and have no faith left in the therapeutic process. There is a point to this question, and it will be addressed throughout the DBT journey; that point is figuring out what will truly make them happy and their life worth living in a more productive way. Not half-heartedly, not numbing their emotions using compulsive behaviors, or moving from one crisis to the next and feeling bad about themselves. But with dedication and wholeness.

According the DBT premise, much of this involves embracing the ideal of holding onto their dreams. Here's why

1. **It gives them hope.** There are some people who know exactly what they want to achieve from their therapy. But

for many, especially those with more severe conditions shrouded in a black-and-white mindset, such as BPD, this isn't feasible. That's why their DBT therapist works with them to dream that another life path is possible. Individuals stuck in their mindset that nothing will get better believe that DBT won't help them since nothing else has worked for them before. Or they've tried making changes on their own, but they haven't been able to keep things working. They're in a place where they relate previously failed attempts at getting better only resulted in them falling flat on their faces, and those feelings of hopelessness are difficult to get over. But with the help of a DBT therapist they've made a connection with, they'll be encouraged to say their dreams out loud or even writing them down, which will give them some much-needed hope. DBT therapists instill that hope opens the heart and mind to accept change. It's what makes them know they *will* feel better, and they deserve to. Most importantly, hope comforts them that they're *not* hopeless and can heal.

2. **Teaches and strengthens resilience.** We've discussed the importance of resilience earlier. In DBT, this skill is what breaks through the belief that our loved one in care can be helped, but they need to understand it takes a great

deal of hard work. DBT challenges individuals at their very core. It makes them face things they've always avoided and tests their patience. It's also the realization that change is slow and, at times, downright scary. But by reminding them of what they're working towards, their goals and dreams of that new life will be what moves them forward, even on days when all they want to do is run away.

3. **Organizes priorities in the most productive way.** The DBT therapist works one-on-one with our loved one in care to help structure their wants, needs, and goals in a more manageable way. When they're struggling with trying to change multiple things at the same time, it's important that they voice those struggles with their therapist before becoming too overwhelmed to see things straight. By having weekly "follow ups" in terms of wants and dreams, the individual will be able to help their therapist know what area to focus on more. For example, the thoughts, behaviors, and feelings currently interfering with their ability of moving forward should be more of a top priority. But, making that clear with the DBT therapist helps reduce those overwhelming emotions, and assure our loved one that they're taking the essential baby steps in making their dreams a reality.

The whole reason our loved one is in DBT is not only to learn what will make them live a happier and more productive life, but also to know it's within their grasp. It's a reality, and one we, as their strongest supporters, know and that their DBT therapist will help them embrace. We just have to get them to see and believe it for themselves.

Effective Ways to Use DBT Skills: DEAR MAN, Accepting Reality, and Mindfulness

In the first two chapters, we discussed the four main groups of skills individuals learn in the DBT program. The main groups include emotional regulation, distress tolerance, mindfulness, and interpersonal effectiveness. DBT therapists focus on specific skill sets within each of these categories, but the base of all areas in DBT is acceptance: accepting people for who they are, seeing situations in the right perspective, and learning how to best communicate wants and needs.

We've used many DBT acronyms to help emphasize points, as well as to make the skills more doable. DEAR MAN is one of the most important DBT skills taught because it helps individuals learn effective ways to ask for things they want, need, or in creating those much-needed boundaries. Another aspect is understanding the importance of reality acceptance, which helps individuals see a situation the way it really is and respond to distress in a more effective way. In this section, we're going to go deeper into these approaches.

DEAR MAN:

This is a subskill of the interpersonal effectiveness DBT skill group. It teaches individuals the best ways to resolve conflict, communicate wants/needs, or make a request as respectfully and effectively as possible. DEAR MAN helps those who normally struggle with maintaining their relationships due to a lack of solid interpersonal skills. Here's how it breaks down:

Describe the situation at hand as simply as possible. The person doesn't put any emotions, explanations, or asks for anything. All a person does here is present the facts that the conversation will stem from.

Express thoughts/feelings using "I" statements. The idea here is to emit a sense of onus on the self so that the other person doesn't immediately slip into defense mode. This is the opportunity to make feelings clear about the situation just described. That way, the person presenting the subject at hand has the chance to express their feelings, and the other person can understand where they're coming from.

Assert request or decision confidently, but respectfully. This is where the individual makes their request or says no to a request made of them. There's no beating around the bush or floating around the subject.

Reinforce the request and why it's being made (or why the answer is no). All relationships are built on some sense of give-and-take. In other words, both sides benefit in some way from the relationship itself. This is a natural, often unspoken, component of interpersonal connections. If someone does us a favor, we're more likely to do them a favor in return. One of the main ideas behind the DEAR MAN skill is reminding the individuals involved that there's something in it for them as well, and it can even help strengthen the relationship.

Mindfulness. This is a reminder for the person to remain mindful of the situation, and not to become distracted by things inside (thoughts or emotions) or around them. It's important to be focused on the conversation at hand, even if the other person becomes defensive. Ensure that the conversation stays on track, despite anything else happening. For those who've struggled with being easily distracted, especially in uncomfortable or emotionally triggering situations, it can be difficult when the conversation gets off track. When that happens, the person decreases the chances of getting what they're asking for. Remembering to stay focused until a resolution has been made increases the odds of success.

Appear confident, even when we don't feel strong. Body

language is very important and exudes confidence we may not have at the moment. Actions like standing or sitting up straight, making direct eye contact, and speaking loudly and clearly all give off a sense of confidence. These things will be difficult for many individuals who struggle with things like eye contact, but it does get easier with practice.

Negotiate when things don't come to a resolution right away. There could be times when the other person may not be on board with our request or will even try negotiating an alternative approach to resolution. A big part of interpersonal effectiveness is understanding the willingness to meet in the middle so that both sides leave the conversation feeling that they walk away with a benefit of some kind. The whole idea is to hear each other out and accommodate each person. The openness to negotiate shows that each person mutually respects each other's feelings and opinions.

These skills help to move through any conversation a little more easily. When each person understands the other's side of a situation, even when things are hard to talk about or face, the result is less misunderstanding, less arguments, and a higher level of understanding.

Reality Acceptance:

When we understand that DBT was established specifically to

help those living with BPD, discussing the area of reality acceptance makes more sense. Those with mental health conditions, such as BPD, don't always perceive a situation the true way that it is. This group of individuals are highly sensitive people who learn distress tolerance skills that help them to cope with uncomfortable and/or painful situations. Specifically in the case of those learning to live with BPD, eating disorders, or other emotionally based conditions, they learn to manage their urges to engage in harmful behaviors. That's the whole point of reality acceptance.

This is a subskill of distress tolerance which has been divided into crisis survival techniques, sensory body awareness, and reality acceptance. All skills learned in the distress tolerance category help a person lower their level of distress in certain situations, so they don't explode out of control resorting to familiar self-destructive coping methods. In this section, we'll focus on the importance of reality acceptance.

Every person experiences pain in their life, whether physically or emotionally. Pain is a natural response that signals something is wrong. It doesn't feel good no matter how it's presented, but the way we choose to deal with it impacts our overall well-being. When individuals choose to ignore their pain or use unhealthy ways to temporarily re-direct their discomfort, that results in ongoing distress. Typically, most people respond to pain in one of four ways:

1. **Problem solving**: This is when a person accepts the reality of the situation and does what's in their power to change, alleviate, or leave that situation.

2. **Changing their feelings:** This means the person understands the given issue, tries to find some kind of meaning, then seeks positivity from the negative.

3. **Acceptance:** Recognizing reality without approving the experience. It means we accept that something we face may be difficult, but it doesn't mean we have to enjoy it or allow it to go on.

4. **Staying in a miserable mindset:** By not accepting reality, individuals choose to go on suffering, which can make an already difficult and stressful situation feel worse.

The only logical and positive way to end the suffering that happens as a result of pain and non-acceptance is to accept reality and face the pain head-on. DBT teaches our loved ones in care three sets of reality acceptance skills that will help them find personal resolution from their suffering.

- **Radical acceptance:** This is when a person stops fighting to see the reality of a situation at hand and responds to it through impulsive or self-harming ways. When something isn't going exactly how they planned, they need to learn to let go of barriers that keep them trapped in their cycle of suffering. To help our loved ones truly accept reality, they need to see the facts about events from their past, even if they may be uncomfortable or undesirable and stop allowing them to control their present. That's the whole point of learning mindfulness, which we'll go into more detail in the next chapter. By analyzing events or situations that have caused them pain and seeing how they've come to interfere with effectively living their present life, they'll begin to move forward with a life worth living, even when pain may arise. This gives them the power to break the cycle of their suffering, unhappiness, bitterness, anger, shame, guilt, or other negative emotions that have held them back from experiencing true happiness. Once individuals are able to accept reality, while disapproving of it at the same time, change can be made. This may sound strange initially, but the entire idea of the DBT approach is embracing the opposite sides of reality: acceptance and change.

- **Altering the mind:** This is the level where an individual must make a choice between turning their mind to focus from staying in their painful place to accepting a situation as it is. Making the inner choice to develop a plan to move to a future of accepting reality and change is when we find our inner peace. Once we are strong enough to turn our minds, we are choosing to take another step towards feeling better.

- **Willingness:** Another point of reality acceptance is being willing and ready to participate fully in life and living. This is another aspect of the mindfulness mindset. Showing willingness is a sign that we're wholeheartedly doing what we need to make our lives better. This can be seen in different ways. Being willing may look like refusing to give up, not allowing ourselves to succumb to usual harmful tactics, or giving up the need of staying in control and fixing every situation. It gives power back to the individual to truly be at peace with reality.

The DBT approach helps individuals regulate their emotions, as well as learn more effective responses to stimuli in their environment. There are some ways to help our loved ones in therapy to practice radical acceptance with their DBT skills at home:

- Help them to acknowledge that they're fighting their reality. ("It shouldn't be like this.")

- Help to remind them that unpleasant realities can't be

changed.

- Help them work through what led to the moment at hand.

- Work with them to practice acceptance not only with their mind, but also with their body and spirit. In other words, remind them to be mindful.

- Have them list, verbally or in writing, what a behavior would look like if they accepted the facts at hand, then ask how they'd respond appropriately.

- Work with them to plan ahead on stress/emotional-triggering events and have them find the best ways they should cope.

- Remind them to be mindful of physical sensations, such as tension, breathing, or heart rate.

- Have them acknowledge and embrace any negative feelings, such as disappointment, anger, shame, or sadness.

- Remind them that life is worth living, even when there might be temporary pain.

- As a last resort, they can write out pros and cons to realize the full impact of any choice or decision.

There are other strategies that we'll go over in the next chapter, but these are a few ideas specific to distress tolerance.

Five Ways to Put DBT Mindfulness Into Action

Mindfulness is probably the biggest and most important part of the DBT program. In the next chapter, we're going to go into greater deal about specific strategies and tips on making mindfulness a part of everyday life, but also why it's so important to our loved ones in DBT. For now, we're going to make this simple by talking about the five specific areas of DBT mindfulness, and a few ways to help our loved ones apply them in their everyday life when they're at home.

The most important DBT mindfulness skills are

- Observe: Observing everything going on around us by increasing our awareness.

- Describe: Once we're able to observe what's outside of ourselves, we should describe the things that trigger our sensory systems and how they make us feel.

- Participate: This basically involves giving a task at hand our full attention and only doing one task at a time. This is also known as being "present," which is a main component in mindfulness.

- Accept: We talked about this in the last section, but it means accepting what is in front of us in a given moment with no judgement or opinion.

- Evolve: Recognize when something isn't working and be willing to try something else.

Our loved one is learning these skills with their DBT therapist, and they need to be given opportunities to put them into practice. Not everything will feel natural to our loved one, as they've been practicing more maladaptive ways of coping. But we can give them many ways to try out what they're learning in non-therapeutic settings until they do feel more second nature.

- **Walking:** We can involve any or all of the above skills. It's important, though, to have our loved one walk in a state of mindfulness without feeling the need to do more than walk, observe, describe, and participate. Walk without judgment.

- **Eating With Meaning:** Eating is a multi-sensory action, so they should enjoy the entire experience of eating for what it truly is. Have them participate in the planning, shopping, cooking, eating, and even the clean-up.

- **Breathing With Purpose:** Breathing is a necessity in life, but it can also be used as a therapeutic tool when done with purpose. It can be calming, soothing, and mind-clearing. These can be done together between you and your loved one, or while you're nearby:

○ Timed Breathing: Inhale for a predetermined amount of time, hold it for about six seconds, then take another six seconds to release the breath.

○ Belly Breathing: Have the person lie or sit where they'll have good back support. Get them to put both hands on their abdomen and direct them to focus on how the belly expands when they inhale.

○ Deep Breathing: This is similar to timed breathing but without set times for inhaling and exhaling. This is one usually practiced when faced with stress, distress, or emotional triggers. Have them draw in deep, long slow inhales through the nose, then match it with long, slow exhales through the mouth.

● **Appreciating:** The whole idea with this one is to fully absorb ourselves in an event in front of us. Suggest choosing a favorite movie or song, then have them experience it as if it were the first time. Challenge them to see or hear new aspects of it, or even have them imagine being right there on the movie set or recording studio. This exercise puts our view in another person's perspective to give a new, fresh appreciation of the whole scene.

These are a few suggestions to help our loved one practice what they're learning. In our next chapter, we'll be putting everything all together in a holistic approach to the DBT method.

CHAPTER 6

Putting it All Together: The

Holistic Approach

You don't have to struggle in silence. You can be un-silent.
You can live well with a mental health condition, as long as
you open up to somebody about it, because it's really
important you share your experience with people so that you
can get the help that you need.

–Demi Lovato

DBT is a solid example of a therapy program that takes a holistic approach. Every person brought into this form of therapy is seen as a unique individual who has their own unique makeup. We have different elements that, *together*, make us the being we are. The main goal of DBT is to help people unite those elements so they can be and live as a whole person. That is a huge goal when you realize that most people coming to the DBT table are fragmented and unable to see themselves in a positive light.

DBT therapists embrace the importance of holistic wellness by helping people see all sides of themselves, and teaching skills to promote healing. To guide individuals to that point, they also guide individuals to have a stronger sense of personal accountability, self-regulation, and responsible decision-making.

One area of focus for this chapter is the mental toughness mindset. There are specific components of being mentally tough that are parallel to those in DBT, especially the areas of emotional intelligence and mindfulness. In a sense, DBT therapists want individuals in their care to become as mentally tough as they can. We'll highlight things people with this mindset have, and a few things they don't, that make them able to take on any challenge they face.

Mindfulness is a main component of DBT, and probably the most difficult group of skills for many individuals. Those who live with BPD, for example, understand the concepts of living in the moment, but their black-and-white way of seeing the world is a major barrier for them to embrace the concept of mindfulness. We're going to discuss how we can help our loved ones in care practice their mindful skills each day, which includes some techniques, activities, and exercises to give a try.

Finally, we'll share a few specific DBT skills to manage stress more effectively. After all, there will be times when our loved one is faced with a stressful or anxiety-triggering situation, and neither their DBT therapist nor a trusted support person will be right there to guide them through. Having skills they can put into motion in those times will increase their sense of inner strength, which is a goal for DBT therapists.

Treating and Caring for the WHOLE Self

Simply put, holistic therapy is a body-centered psychotherapy that brings together traditional and non-traditional treatments, so an individual is helped as a whole being at a deeper level. This approach means that the focus of healthcare isn't on one specific area, but considers the mental, physical, and spiritual elements that affect a person's well-being.

DBT is considered a form of a holistic approach because it combines talk therapy with being conscious of how our minds affect our bodies. Generally, people seek out these forms of therapies to deal with stress, tension, or to increase their overall health. For those in DBT, however, it's a way to be more emotionally regulated and to help individuals function more effectively in stress or emotionally charged events. The most important benefit for those in DBT in considering holistic approaches is that it empowers them to prepare or recognize triggers in a situation before it has a chance to impact them.

Some research does suggest that integrated, holistic care can have many benefits, such as

- Offering physical and mental benefits that are also affordable

- Reducing anxiety and stress

- Being easily incorporated into various purposes and situations

- Helping to improve sleep and mood, decrease stress, and improve relaxation

- Increasing both physical and mental health

Many of the practices in the holistic approach are considered branches of complementary and alternative medicine (CAM). These practices support the mind, body, and spirit connection, and some examples of the top ones include

- **Acupuncture:** This may not be everyone's cup of tea as it involves needles. It's a Chinese practice where fine needles are inserted through the skin at specific points with the focus of curing disease or relieving pain.

- **Biofeedback:** This non-invasive practice is a way to learn to control some of the body's functions during stress or anxiety-triggered situations. During a session, a person is connected to electrical sensors that receive information about how the body is reacting to certain stimuli. The point is if we can make a connection between certain situations and our body's reaction to them, we can intervene with more effective coping methods.

- **Breathwork:** The idea of breathwork is focusing entirely on breathing and its calming effects on the body. It helps to reduce usual acute stress response and elicits the body's relaxation response through deep abdominal breathing. It often confused with meditation, which is more about increasing awareness of how the body operates. Breathwork, on the other hand, is a form of *active* meditation where breathing is used to alter our mood, perspective, and reactions.

- **Guided Imagery:** This practice helps people divert their focus in stressful moments to positive images in their minds. When we turn our heads and think "happy thoughts" when getting blood drawn, for example, this is a form of guided imagery. When done with a therapeutic professional, people are taught to reach a relaxed, focused state to help them reduce stress and give them a sense of well-being.

- **Massage:** For those who are able to handle more touch-focused therapies, this is a beneficial practice. There are several types of massage, depending on what exactly a person's goal is, but the main idea is manipulating the muscles using hands or instruments for relaxation, kneading out stress, or a non-medicinal way to deal with injury.

- **Meditation:** As touched on above, meditation is a powerful practice of activating and maintaining the mind-body connection. Meditation can elicit a deep state of relaxation and a peaceful mind. While meditating, a person focuses their attention on eliminating the jumbled thoughts that overload their mind and causes them stress. A good way to look at it is that we're trying to expel the bad and bring in the good.

- **Reiki:** This is another form of touch-therapy, but on a much less intense level than massage. It's more of an energy-healing practice that increases relaxation, reduces stress and anxiety, and realigns the body's energy pathways through gentle touch. Practitioners use their hands to bring energy into the body, as well as to improve the flow and balance of the body's energy to increase inner healing.

- **Tai Chi:** This is one of various practices where deliberate breathing and movement work in unison to promote inner peace. It involves a series of gentle physical exercises and stretches where each posture flows into the next, ensuring that the body stays in constant motion. It helps to promote serenity through gentle movements and breathing, ideally connecting the mind and body.

- **Yoga:** The premise of this practice is similar to tai chi in that breathing and body movement are connected. The main difference is that in yoga, a pose is held for specific amounts of time while focusing on breathing, with a break in between each pose. The connection of mind, body, and spirit is the same but there is an added benefit of endurance, flexibility, and strength.

These are only a few of the many holistic or alternative practices available. The best approach is to discuss with the DBT therapist and primary healthcare provider in terms of overall health goals, tolerance levels of sensory input (e.g., some forms of touch therapy may not be the best for those adverse to touch), and the individual needs of the person in care.

The Dos and Don'ts of Being Mentally Tough

Mental toughness isn't a mindset we're born with, but there are specific traits that those high in mental toughness have in common. And when we look closely at those who possess these traits, we can see they're very similar to skills DBT therapists are trying to teach individuals in their care:

- **Delayed Gratification:** This is the conscious act of resisting the impulse jumping on an immediate reward with the hope of gaining a more beneficial reward down the road. The main goal of learning delayed gratification is essential to self-regulation or self-control.

- **Focusing on What Is Controllable:** This is a DBT skill known as *radical acceptance*, which we'll go into more detail about in a separate section. For mentally tough people, this is seen as not wasting time worrying about what *might* happen, but more on what they *can make* happen.

- **Not Worrying About Controlling Others:** As an extension of the above point, mentally tough people don't worry about controlling others. They know they have absolutely no power over other people, only on how they respond to others and their own actions.

- **Seeing the Past Only in the Capacity of a Learning Tool:** As we've touched on several times in earlier chapters, if we allow the past to bleed into the present, we'll remain stationary. The past is valuable and meaningful, and we can learn many things from it, but it shouldn't define who we are or the direction we're meant to go in. When we make mistakes, or things don't quite go the way we plan, we should see it as an opportunity to improve. That's a forward-thinking view that is highly regarded in DBT as well.

- **Celebrating Other People's Success:** Before many individuals go into DBT, they're stuck in the mindset that they're failures, no good, or worthless. These negative thoughts will sink in deeper if someone succeeds at something they weren't able to do. The whole point of letting go of those ideas is that it's a great thing when other people do well, and we should join in their celebration. We could learn something from that person that we could embrace to expand our own success. There's no room for jealousy or resentment in a mentally tough person's life.

- **Not Jumping on the Pity Train:** It's one thing to vent and get things off our chest, but it's another to stay on that platform and use it as an excuse for not making progress. The energy it takes to complain, criticize, or beat ourselves up could be better spent on finding a solution to the problem at hand.

- **Believing in Themselves:** In a nutshell, a person who is mentally tough pays less attention to what others are doing and saying and focuses more on themselves and their goals. Essentially, they seek genuine relationships with others and aren't "people pleasers."

- **Being Grateful:** Mentally tough people aren't worried about what they *don't* have or what they *haven't* achieved. They embrace all they have, those they have near them, and feel blessed to be able to have goals to keep reaching for. They are inspired for all they have in their lives, however small.

Those who are mentally tough also focus on eliminating negative habitual behaviors that interfere with their natural sense of resilience and inner strength. Each of us has an innate drive to want to do better, to be happier living our lives, and to find solutions to existing problems. What many of us tend to do is clog up the process by over-thinking, allowing negative self-talk to sneak in, and not having clear priorities.

If we work through these negativities, and it's a good portion of what DBT therapists try navigating individuals through, we may realize we're more mentally tough than we thought. Here are a few don'ts to help our loved on in therapy embrace the concept of mental toughness:

- **Don't over-think.** This may be easier said than done for those who have severe anxiety or conditions that are emotionally based. It's one thing to plan, problem-solve, and think about a situation from different angles, but when do we tell ourselves that all of those thoughts floating in our head are doing more damage than good? If we could picture it, we're building worry on top of worry, and *that's* why we become overwhelmed. It's okay to have ideas and thoughts but having a good filter to eliminate those that aren't working for us or have no real connection to a situation at hand, will help us turn our focus on the best direction.

- **Don't beat ourselves up as a motivation tactic.** This point may not seem like it needs to be expanded on, but it's important to understand. When someone close to us makes a poor choice, or something doesn't work out as they planned, our immediate reaction is to reach out and offer our support. They may cut themselves right down, but we do everything to lift them up so they can keep going. Why is it so easy for us to be compassionate, supportive, and motivating to our friend in need, but we aren't able to do the same thing for ourselves in a similar scenario? One of the main things a DBT therapist works on with people in their care is to help them re-build themselves from the inside out. Being kind to ourselves, especially during tough times, is what pulls us through. *That* is more motivational than to rip ourselves apart, which only keeps us in that negative place.

- **Don't prioritize based on results.** This is another huge skill set that DBT therapists work on individuals with. People who are mentally tough don't base their success on *results,* but more on the effort they put into the task. Trying to be perfect or the best at everything only leads to disappointment, as well as is a serious kick to our self-worth. The idea of perfection isn't real or achievable and is often an expectation we put on ourselves. Having smaller, attainable goals help to build confidence, self-esteem, and self-worth.

- **Don't be afraid of being alone once in a while.** The idea of being alone with personal thoughts is actually a highly stressful thing. For those who have conditions like BPD, for example, being alone can be a terrifying thing because they become consumed in the cycle of "feeling-thinking-doing" that they don't believe they can control. It takes time to absorb what their DBT therapist is teaching them about not allowing their minds to be taken over by emotions or moods they don't understand. Being alone from time to time is a great way to figure those things out, but what exactly is meant by having "quality alone time"? The idea is to work with the mind rather than succumb to it, which means making the time to understand thinking patterns and emotional responses. What triggers them? What's going on when we feel/think that way? What are the best ways to deal with them that won't make things worse? That means that rather than avoiding, escaping, or otherwise running away from emotions or thoughts, we need to get to know them.

Being more mentally tough takes time to nurture and grow, but it becomes easier the more opportunities a person in DBT care has to practice the skills they're learning.

Putting Mindfulness into Practice by Embracing Radical Acceptance

Radical acceptance is part of the group of skills learned in the distress tolerance module of the DBT program. Generally, this is the skill we learn that helps prevent painful occurrences in life from turning into suffering. This isn't to say that we need to "suck it up" and just accept that painful event and move on. It's more about recognizing that the facts of a situation are what they are and fighting those facts won't change the reality itself.

In other words, we learn to embrace the "It is what it is" mindset.

DBT teaches ways to acknowledge an event for what it was and the way it made us feel, but not to allow that event to become a long-term, enduring thing. To be clear, radical acceptance isn't about approval. It's about accepting with our whole self that even when we don't like the present facts, it isn't within our control to change them. The best way to clarify the concept of radical acceptance is going over the steps involved as laid out by the founder of DBT, Marsha Linehan:

- Acknowledge that we're questioning something about present facts or reality.

- Remember that the current situation is the way it's going to be and that we can't change it.

- Tell ourselves that other events caused the one at hand and acknowledge them.

- Put the holistic approach into play by accepting the facts with the mind, body, and spirit (e.g., positive self-talk, guided imagery, or mindfulness).

- List the behaviors we'd engage in as if we accept the situation the way it is, then carry them out.

- Describe how it would feel to accept what we believe isn't acceptable about a given situation, and what would happen.

- Pay close attention to the sensations that come up when we think about the things we need to accept.

- Allow the emotions like anger, disappointment, or sadness stemming from the present situation to come to the surface, rather than muffle them.

- Acknowledge that our life can be worth living even when we experience painful times.

- If we sense we're fighting radical acceptance, list the pros and cons and continue trying.

This is a difficult skill to embrace, but it can be very effective in helping those we love in care to move out of their black-and-white mindset they've kept close for so long.

Mindfulness Exercises for Depression, Anger, Addiction and Anxiety

Although DBT was specifically created to help those with BPD and similar diagnoses, the skills can be helpful to many of us for learning to cope with stress, anxiety and emotionally charged situations.

In this final section, we're going to focus on exercises and activities that can be used for those living with depression, anger, and anxiety. The skills also work well for those trying to stay on track after recovering from addiction. It should be noted at this point that a person living with BPD has several of these conditions to cope with on top of several other symptoms. But an individual can be struggling in one specific area and still benefit from the following activities.

Depression: When focusing specifically on depression, mindfulness can significantly reduce the symptoms as well as lower the risk of debilitating relapse. For these individuals, there are three keys in making mindfulness a successful component in their treatment:

- It helps to teach the person to be present in the moment. That gives them a moment to think about what they're feeling and thinking right then and choose the best response in that moment.

- It teaches the person that it's okay to say "no," and that having strong boundaries will give them balance and boost their confidence.

- Most importantly, it teaches them to be present in their relationships and helps them to communicate and connect with the other person.

The body scan and intentional breathing discussed in earlier chapters work best with those learning to cope with depression. These techniques keep them in the present, and to deal with situations, events, and people *in the now.*

Anger: Mindfulness is an effective tool to manage anger. When we think about it, anger is the most reactive and immediate emotional response and seems to be the closest to the surface. Most of us are able to put it aside, and deal with a situation or triggers more logically. Others, though, aren't in control of this negative and potentially harmful emotion, and mindfulness can help with this.

When deep breathing, guided imagery or similar calming activities aren't effective, the following DBT technique focusing on mindfulness may help:

- Have the person sit in a comfortable position in a chair or on the floor and have them close their eyes. Ask them to pay close attention to the areas of their body that are touching the cushion/chair/floor or whatever they're sitting on.

- Get them to draw in a deep breath until their lungs feel full, then quickly exhale.

- Ask them to think back to a time when they felt angry,

choosing a milder or quickly resolved time. Then ask them to experience the anger they felt in that moment, reminding them to remove all other emotions felt at the time like shame, guilt, or sadness.

- From there, ask them to turn their focus on the way their body responded to the anger. Have them describe sensations such as coldness, warmth, numbness, etc.

- The next step may be difficult for them but have them express compassion for the anger. It might help to remind them that anger is a normal human emotion we all have at some point and to view it as something they'd help another person work through in a similar situation. The idea in this point is to deal with it with understanding and love.

- Bring the focus back to breathing and keep them there until the emotions have settled down and subsided. Then have them let the anger go, or actually say goodbye to it. It may feel strange to do this, but it's a way to close the door on it.

- Once the door is shut on the anger in that moment, have them reflect on it. Ask them to go over the emotions they felt, the way they effected their body, how they worked through it, and how they showed compassion for their anger so it could be let go. This is an important step because it will help them turn to this if/when a situation arises that brings the anger up again.

Anxiety: Mindfulness is a way to help regulate moods and to help individuals re-focus their thoughts. Those trapped in an anxiety-triggered mindset can literally go from coping to explosive to acting on impulses within minutes. The idea of implementing mindfulness is to intervene at the level of moving out of coping before it has a chance to reach explosive. The following skills are strengthened through learning mindfulness and are the base of helping a person cope with their anxiety:

- **Volition/Intention:** This is the base of all other skills because individuals need to focus on their intention of working through their anxiety.

- **Beginner's Mind:** It means the person has to have a willingness to see things from a new perspective and embrace new ideas in dealing with their anxiety.

- **Patience:** This is a big skill to put into practice, especially for individuals who aren't able to see that gray area. Learning this skill helps to expand their point of view and to help them persevere when they face hurdles.

- **Acknowledgement:** Being able to learn to take each

experience we come across as it is means that we accept what's happening in a moment and know that it will pass.

- **Nonjudgmental:** This skill involves dealing with a present experience without evaluating or judging it. It involves letting go of our judgment of ourselves, our feelings and thoughts, so that we can move forward from a more balanced perspective.

- **Unchanging:** This refers to being able to view a situation as it is without trying to change it. It involves accepting their current state of mind.

- **Self-Reliance:** The skill of trusting the self as well as being able to handle our feelings is an essential goal in DBT. Strengthening these skills helps an individual acknowledge, experience, and let go of anxiety.

- **Allowing:** This works with the point of unchanging in that an individual learns that it takes less energy to learn to work with anxiety than it does to fight or hide it.

- **Self-Compassion:** This point was touched on earlier in dealing with anger. In expressing compassion, understanding, and support to the self, we'll be in a better place to deal with our anxiety. It also helps us to allow others in to remind us of our coping skills.

139

- **Balance:** Learning these skills will help individuals open their perspective and understanding that a whole experience goes beyond their present feelings, good or bad.

Anxiety is as tough to understand from an outside view as it is for the person experiencing it. But learning to cope with anxiety by embracing the above skills has more benefits than can be listed here. The simplest way of applying mindfulness to anxiety is reminding the individual to focus on bodily sensations when they experience anxiety, stay present in that moment, and allow themselves to think about the feelings or distressing thought that arise in that moment.

The whole point is that when the individual can see their thoughts for what they are, and that most of the time they aren't true or highly exaggerated, the easier it will be to release them.

Addiction: As discussed in earlier chapters, addictions are maladaptive coping methods many individuals turn to before finally embracing a form of therapy. It's an easier to self-medicate than it is to face up to what we're trying to distract ourselves from. DBT can be very effective in conjunction with the other methods of addiction treatment.

Mindfulness can increase the number and strength of connections in the brain that make us more aware of our bodily sensations, as well as being highly effective with helping to regulate emotions. It also helps individuals recognize, tolerate, and cope with their negative emotions. Plus, it helps ward off cravings. The whole idea with addiction is that we've taught the brain to want and need the substance, then we "un-learn" but replacing the substance with more positive practices and working through cravings using the same steps as would be used in working through anger.

Chapter Summary

Each chapter covers a vast amount of information, some of which can be overwhelming. There may be times when you need to take a break to digest ideas, which is totally understandable. To make it easier to maneuver through each discussion, or to return to concepts or ideas later on, we've broken the chapters down into brief summaries.

Chapter One: DBT if often the "one last try" for many families in searching for the right therapy for a loved one, and this chapter covers everything a person needs and wants to know about DBT. The discussion focuses on the history of the therapy, the different areas covered, and the expectations of DBT therapists as well as those in their care. The number one question asked in any therapy is whether it's right for the individual, and we discuss how to know.

Chapter Two: This chapter delves deeper into the DBT program. We discuss the different individuals on the DBT team and what their roles are. The chapter takes a closer look at the structure of the program including descriptions of the four DBT modules, the essential skills individuals will learn, and helpful strategies to help the individual to keep moving forward through the program.

Chapter Three: Although DBT was created specifically to help those diagnosed with Borderline Personality Disorder (BPD), the skills and exercises taught in the program can help individuals who struggle with several other mental health conditions. The focus of discussion for this chapter is to show how DBT is a multifaceted form of therapy that can go beyond its main focus.

Chapter Four: One of the most important people on the DBT team are those closest to them who will be a part of their life outside of the therapeutic setting, such as family, friends, and other loving supporters. This chapter is all about ways to help loved ones in DBT at home, in their community, and in their regular lives. There's a standalone section on what strategies supporters can do when the person in care fights being helped.

Chapter Five: One of the main components of DBT is guiding the individual in care to empower themselves enough to advocate for themselves. Self-empowerment and self-advocacy are one of the greatest assets a person living with a mental health condition can have. It builds their confidence, self-esteem, and self-worth so they are never defined by their diagnosis. Loving supporters learn to advocate for the person in care, as they're learning to advocate for themselves.

Chapter Six: Since the mindfulness mindset is a main module in the DBT program, it's already helping individuals embrace a holistic approach to their care. This chapter highlights the importance of self-care and taking care of the whole self, and includes various activities, strategies, and exercises to put the holistic perspective into practice. There are even suggestions for loving supporters to participate right alongside the individual in care.

Conclusion

The best thing you could do is master the chaos in you. You are not thrown into the fire, you are the fire.
–Mama Indigo

Learning to cope in our world at the best of times is difficult enough. Life is an adventure filled with surprises, but it isn't a predictable one. It can be compared to planning a trip around the information we get from the weather network. We set a plan, prepare ourselves for what we're told to expect, and do our best for any possible deviations from the forecast. Like the weather, though, life is unpredictable, and we can't be prepared for every single "what if" that may (or may not) come up. For those living with mental health conditions, life feels that way every day.

When a person has been physically injured or born with some sort of physical hurdle, we can be empathetic because we can see it. Even if a person has some sort of physical disease or medical condition that is easily understood or relatable, we can have compassion. So why aren't those living with mental health conditions, that are often debilitating, offered the same empathetic support? This lack of willingness to understand is the main reason many people don't seek help when they need it. Even in our modern times, the stigma placed on those struggling with mental health issues stands in the way of those people reaching out, or even believing there is effective help and support for them when they are brave enough to reach out. That's where DBT steps in.

DBT therapists don't focus on *curing* individuals, but on recognizing what's already within a person that can be nurtured and strengthened. Every person is treated as the unique individual they are and taught vital skills to guide them to all they're meant to be. The DBT program is all about acceptance, self-regulation, and embracing change as it happens. It's about stopping the negative self-talk tapes and creating new ones that are positive. It's about dissolving maladaptive coping methods and replacing them with more effective tools that rebuild their inner strength. It's about acknowledging that gray area they usually ignored, moving them out beyond the black-and-white thinking that's held them back. Finally, it's about facing the things they feared the most, rather than bury them, so they learn to finally be happy, productive, and at peace.

These are all difficult, new, and often terrifying things for those who have actively avoided them for so long. But once they see the focus isn't on changing the individual, but more on changing the way they perceive the world around them and how they fit into it, they'll gravitate to the positive light of hope. That doesn't mean the journey will be an easy one.

DBT therapists take a tremendous amount of care and responsibility in what they do. They take the time not only to understand every individual brought under their care, but how to create a care plan specific to that person's needs. They understand that the therapeutic team doesn't just involve the specialists, but also includes the loving supporters and the individual themself. It's the combined efforts and insight of every person around the DBT team table who helps the individual get past their barriers and finally see the future ahead with no fear.

The DBT program is very intense with the expectation of putting in the hard work. But the therapists are there every step of the way no matter what hurdles the person in care faces, or how difficult certain things may be to get through. Every effort put in will be rewarded many times over. We hope that within the chapters of this book, the information, strategies, and exercises will enhance what is already being taught, and that loving supporters will feel they're making a solid contribution to their loved one's care.

Above all else, we hope that planning future adventures won't elicit as much fear or anxiety of what surprises may come up, but rather offer more effective tools to wade through any storms with positiveness, acceptance, and the renewed sense of belief that calmer waters are always there after the storm passes.

Thank You

Before you leave, I'd just like to say, thank you so much for purchasing my book.

I spent many days and nights working on this book so I could finally put this in your hands.

So, before you leave, I'd like to ask you a small favor.

Would you please consider posting a review on the platform? Your reviews are one of the best ways to support indie authors like me, and every review counts.

Your feedback will allow me to continue writing books just like this one, so let me know if you enjoyed it and why. I read every review and I would love to hear from you. Simply visit the link below to leave a review.

References

Ackerman, C. E. (2017, January 18). *21 Mindfulness Exercises & Activities For Adults (+ PDF)*. https://positivepsychology.com/mindfulness-exercises-techniques-activities/#mindfulness-depression-anxiety-anger-addictions

Bay Area DBT & Couples Counseling Center. (2017, May 5). *How to begin dreaming: Building a life worth living in DBT* https://bayareadbtcc.com/how-to-begin-dreaming-dbt/

Beltrani, A. (2022). *Pros and Cons of DBT* https://concept.paloaltou.edu/resources/business-of-practice-blog/pros-and-cons-of-dbt

CAMH. Dialectical Behavioural Therapy. (2022). https://www.camh.ca/en/health-info/mental-illness-and-addiction-index/dialectical-behaviour-therapy

Carrico, B. (2021, June 15). *Dialectical Behavior Therapy for Anxiety, Depression, and More*. https://psychcentral.com/lib/dialectical-behavior-therapy-for-more-than-borderline-personality-disorder#recap

Chamberlain, J. (2021). *Holistic Wellness: Caring for the Mind, Body, & Spirit*. https://www.choosingtherapy.com/holistic-wellness/

References

Choosing Therapy. (2020) *DBT for Teens: How It Works, Examples & Effectiveness.* www.choosingtherapy.com/dbt-for-teens/.

CMHA Durham. (2016, April 29). *Advocating for Treatment* https://cmhadurham.ca/finding-help/advocating-for-treatment/

Floyd, E. (2019, October 28). *Accepting Reality Using DBT Skills | Skyland Trail.* Skyland Trail. https://www.skylandtrail.org/accepting-reality-using-dbt-skills/

Haden, J. (2014, July 23). *7 Habits of People With Remarkable Mental Toughness.* https://www.inc.com/jeff-haden/7-habits-of-people-with-remarkable-mental-toughness.html

Harris, A. (2020, April 7). *10 Steps of Radical Acceptance.* https://hopeway.org/blog/radical-acceptance

Linehan, M. (2022). *Boundary Building Skill - Dialectical Behavior Therapy (DBT) Tools.* https://dbt.tools/interpersonal_effectiveness/boundary-building.php

Lorandini, J. (2021, August 8). *5 Ways to Apply DBT Mindfulness Skills in Your Everyday Life* https://suffolkdbtjl.com/5-ways-to-apply-dbt-mindfulness-skills-in-your-everyday-life/

Lorandini, J. (February 2, 2021). *3 Ways Family Involvement in DBT Therapy Makes a Difference* https://suffolkdbtjl.com/3-ways-family-involvement-in-dbt-therapy-makes-a-difference/

Martin, S. (2016, December 9). *How to Stop Enabling.* Psych Central; Psych Central. https://psychcentral.com/blog/imperfect/2016/12/how-to-stop-enabling#Manage-your-anxiety.

Mental Health America. (2021, October 4). *What to do when they don't want help* https://screening.mhanational.org/content/what-do-when-they-dont-want-help/

Petroziello, A. (2020, June 25). *Self Empowerment and Self Advocacy in*

Mental Health. https://eymtherapy.com/blog/self-empowerment-advocacy-mental-health/

Psychotherapy Academy. *The Structure of Standard DBT: The 4 Skill Modules* (2021, October 5). https://psychotherapyacademy.org/dbt/structure-of-standard-dbt/

Skyland Trail Therapy. (2017, August 27). *4 Differences Between CBT and DBT and How to Tell Which is Right for You* https://www.skylandtrail.org/4-differences-between-cbt-and-dbt-and-how-to-tell-which-is-right-for-you/

Sunrise Treatment Center. (April 24, 2017). *Top 5 DBT Skills to Use at Home* https://sunrisertc.com/top-5-dbt-skills-use-home/

Sunrise Residential Treatment Center. (2018, March 26). *The DEAR MAN DBT Skill: The Most Effective Way to Make a Request.* https://sunrisertc.com/dear-man/

Tartakovsky, M. (2021, May 21). *What Is Dialectical Behavior Therapy?* https://psychcentral.com/lib/an-overview-of-dialectical-behavior-therapy#dbt-and-you

Quilter, M. (2020, October 13). *Is DBT Right for Me?* https://www.lifeskillssouthflorida.com/mental-health-blog/is-dbt-right-for-me/

Whyte, A. (2020, May 19). *Family DBT at Evolve: How We Do It.* Evolve Treatment Centers. https://evolvetreatment.com/blog/family-dbt-at-evolve/

Wignall, N. (2020, July 6). *4 Things Mentally Tough People Don't Do.* https://nickwignall.com/mentally-tough-people/